TABLE OF CONTENTS

Belarus	4
Czech Republic	20
Greece	42
Poland	64
Romania	85
Russia	107
Ukraine	127
Answer Key	147
Additional Resources	150

BELARUS

MP5126

PASSPORT SERIES

EASTERN EUROPE AND RUSSIA

Author: Deborah Kopka
Contributors: Ellen M. Dolan (Greece),
  Don McKay (Poland),
  Susan J. Williams (Russia)
Editor: Jonathan Gross
Original Illustrations: Ada K. Hanlon, Kathy Mitter
Design and Layout: Kati Baker

Copyright: 2011 Lorenz Educational Press, a Lorenz company, and its licensors.
All rights reserved.

Permission to photocopy the student activities in this book is hereby granted to one teacher as part of the purchase price. This permission may only be used to provide copies for this teacher's specific classroom setting. This permission may not be transferred, sold, or given to any additional or subsequent user of this product. Thank you for respecting copyright laws.

Printed in the United States of America

ISBN 978-1-4291-2252-8

BRIDGING the Gaps in Education™
Lorenz Educational Press
P.O. Box 802 • Dayton, OH 45401-0802

for other LEP products visit our website
www.LorenzEducationalPress.com

*All statistics are based on information from 2010.
**For further information on pronunciations, research foreign language dictionaries and/or the Internet.

METRIC CONVERSIONS

The purpose of this page is to aid in the conversion of measurements in this book from the English system to the metric system. Note that the tables below show two types of ounces. Liquid ounces measure the volume of liquids and have therefore been converted into milliliters. Dry ounces measure weight and have been converted into grams. Because dry substances such as sugar and flour may have different densities, it is advisable to measure them according to weight rather than volume. The measurement unit of the cup has been reserved solely for liquid, or volume, conversions.

Conversion Formulas

when you know	formula	to find	when you know	formula	to find
teaspoons	× 5	milliliters	milliliters	× .20	teaspoons
tablespoons	× 15	milliliters	milliliters	× .60	tablespoons
fluid ounces	× 29.57	milliliters	milliliters	× .03	fluid ounces
liquid cups	× 240	milliliters	milliliters	× .004	liquid cups
U.S. gallons	× 3.78	liters	liters	× .26	U.S. gallons
dry ounces	× 28.35	grams	grams	× .035	dry ounces
inches	× 2.54	centimeters	centimeters	× .39	inches
square inches	× 6.45	square centimeters	square centimeters	× .15	square inches
feet	× .30	meters	meters	× 3.28	feet
square feet	× .09	square meters	square meters	× 10.76	square feet
yards	× .91	meters	meters	× 1.09	yards
miles	× 1.61	kilometers	kilometers	× .62	miles
square miles	× 2.59	square kilometers	square kilometers	× .40	square miles
Fahrenheit	(°F − 32) × 5/9	Celsius	Celsius	(°C × 9/5) + 32	Fahrenheit

Equivalent Temperatures
- 32°F = 0°C (water freezes)
- 212°F = 100°C (water boils)
- 350°F = 177°C
- 375°F = 191°C
- 400°F = 204°C
- 425°F = 218°C
- 450°F = 232°C

Common Cooking Conversions
- 1/2 cup = 120 milliliters
- 12 fluid ounces = 354.88 milliliters
- 1 quart (32 ounces) = 950 milliliters
- 1/2 gallon = 1.89 liters
- 1 Canadian gallon = 4.55 liters
- 8 dry ounces (1/2 pound) = 227 grams
- 16 dry ounces (1 pound) = 454 grams

WELCOME TO BELARUS!

After seventy years as a republic of the Soviet Union, Belarus (Byel-*uh*-ROOS) has been independent since 1991. However, it still maintains close ties to Russia. In 1999, Belarus and Russia signed a friendship and cooperation pact to maintain their political and economic ties. But neither their governments nor their economies are integrated yet.

The first president of Belarus, Aleksandr Lukashenko, has maintained an extremely tight hand on the country since his election in 1994. Today there continue to be many government restrictions on basic freedoms. As with the old Soviet Union, Belarus is still cloaked in secrecy. People in the West hear little about it. So let's explore!

FAST FACTS

Official Name: Republic of Belarus

Location: Eastern Europe
Belarus is bordered by Russia to the north and east, Ukraine to the south, Poland to the west, and Lithuania and Latvia to the north.

Population: 9,612,632 (2010 estimate)

Capital City: Minsk

Area: 80,155 square miles (2010 estimate); Belarus is a bit smaller than the state of Kansas.

Major Languages: Belarusian
Russian

Major Religion: Eastern Orthodox: 80%
Other (including Roman Catholic, Protestant, Jewish, and Muslim): 20%

Currency: The Belarusian ruble (paper only); 1 ruble = 100 kapeikas (kă-pā-kăs)
There are eleven Belarus bank notes, ranging from 10 rubles to 100,000 rubles. There are no coins in Belarus.

Climate: Cold winters and warm summers. Some parts of Belarus have sub-zero temperatures more than a third of the year.

The Land: Generally flat with much marshland

Type of Government: Presidential Republic

Flag: A red horizontal band at the top signifies past struggles and oppression. Below this is a green horizontal band that is one-half the width of the red band; it represents hope and the country's many forests. The white vertical stripe on the hoist side of the flag has Belarusian national ornamentation in red.

National Emblem:	The National Emblem of Belarus features a ribbon in the colors of the national flag, a map of Belarus, wheat ears, and a red star. At the bottom of the emblem is the name of the country. The elements on the emblem are not tied to any official symbolism.
National Flower: (Unofficial)	Centaurea (basket flower)
National Symbol:	the Stork
Motto:	"Zhive Belarus!" ("Long live Belarus!")

Natural Environment

Belarus is one of only 44 landlocked countries in the world. It has large areas or marshy land, and about 40 percent of it is covered by forests. It has 11,000 lakes and three major rivers: the Neman, the Pripyat, and the Dnepr (nē-per).

Peat, oil and natural gas, granite, limestone, chalk, sand, gravel, and clay are among the natural resources of this country. Unfortunately, about 70 percent of the radiation from the Ukraine's nuclear disaster at Chernobyl Nuclear Power Plant in 1986 (one of the reactors exploded) entered Belarus. As of 2005, about 20 percent of its land (mostly farmland and forests in the southeast) is still contaminated. The agriculture that had once been a part of the country has, in large part, been destroyed.

Plants and Animals

About 80 percent of the plants in Belarus are made up of thousands of species of algae and fungi! In the sky, on the land, and in the water, you'll find 310 species of birds, 13 species of amphibians, 7 species of reptiles, and 46 species of fish that are indigenous to Belarus. Of the 76 types of mammals found in Belarus, the European bison is the best known. It's also the fastest-growing! The country's program to conserve and reintroduce the bison has swelled the number of bison in Belarus to several hundred. Belarus now has the world's largest population of bison.

UNESCO World Heritage Sites in Belarus

Belarus has four UNESCO World Heritage Sites of cultural significance maintained by UNECSO's World Heritage program. These include the Mir Castle Complex (built in the 15th and 16th centuries), the Niasvizh Castle (built in the 16th century), and the Belovezhskaya Puscha (an ancient forest on the border of Belarus and Poland). The fourth site, the Struve Geodetic Arc, is one of a chain of arcs that go through nine other countries; they were used to survey the shape and size of the earth before the age of satellites.

Name _____   Date _____

PLANTS AND ANIMALS OF BELARUS

Belarus is filled with plants and animals! Find them in this word search. The words can be listed across, down, up, or backwards.

ASH	BISON	ELK
HORSE	POTATO	WHEAT
BEAVER	CENTAUREA	FALCON
MUSHROOM	RYE	WILD BOAR
BERRIES	DEER	GOAT
OAK	STORK	WOLF
BIRCH	EAGLE	
PINE	TURKEY	

W	D	C	E	N	T	A	U	R	E	A
I	E	H	A	I	S	J	A	S	M	S
L	B	F	L	O	W	E	S	R	O	H
D	O	K	D	S	H	O	R	P	O	R
B	E	R	R	I	E	S	T	O	R	K
O	L	O	E	Z	A	H	U	T	H	A
A	K	G	O	A	T	N	R	A	S	O
R	E	V	A	E	B	C	K	T	U	D
B	I	S	O	N	L	H	E	O	M	P
F	A	L	C	O	N	R	Y	E	C	I
X	O	P	N	E	O	E	L	R	H	N
B	I	R	C	H	D	E	A	G	L	E
Q	A	K	N	I	T	D	E	I	A	T

MP5126 – Belarus

7

A History of Belarus

Early History

There were probably settlements in Belarus about 10,000 years ago. But recorded history begins with the Baltic and Slavic tribes who settled in the area in the early centuries CE.

The emerging country was absorbed into the Kievan (kē-efun) Rus state about 862 CE near the present-day city of Novgorod in northwestern Russia. Belarus later became part of what was called Litva, which included modern Belarus and Lithuania. Belarus was the birthplace of the Grand Duchy of Lithuania—a state that became the largest in Europe by the 14th century. Belarusian was the state language of the Grand Duchy until 1697.

Decades of Turmoil

The Russian Empire occupied Belarus from the end of the 18th century until 1918. In March of 1918, Belarus declared itself a National Republic. But it wasn't one for long! The Bolshevik revolutionaries forcibly absorbed it into what became the Soviet Union. In 1922, it became a founding member of the Soviet Union.

In the 1930s, Belarus suffered severely under Joseph Stalin, the Soviet Union's brutal dictator. Stalin ordered the execution of 100,000 Belarusian intellectuals, political opponents, and others. Thousands more were sent to labor camps in Siberia, the eastern region of current-day Russia where criminals were punished with imprisonment.

Belarus fared little better in the 1940s. Nazi Germany invaded it in World War II. During the Nazi occupation from 1941 to 1944, Germany severely damaged the Belarusian infrastructure, economy, and national spirit. The capital of Minsk was almost completely destroyed. Some 2.2 million people were killed (about a third of the population), which included most of the country's Jews. The population did not regain its pre-World War II levels until 1971. Many villages were burned. The country also lost half of its economic resources. In 1944, the Soviet Red Army drove the Germans out of Belarus. The outcome of World War II established the country's present borders.

Belarus was among the founders of the United Nations in 1945 and began to work toward rebuilding the Soviet Union. It became a major manufacturing center that brought many ethnic Russians into the country for jobs in the factories. Stalin began the "Sovietization" of Belarus to isolate it as much as possible from the West. He placed Russians from various parts of the Soviet Union in the Belarusian government. Severe restrictions were placed on speaking the Belarusian language and observing its customs. Stalin's successor, Nikita Krushchev, continued this policy.

The Chernobyl Disaster

In 1986, Belarus was heavily affected by radioactive fallout from the nuclear explosion at Chernobyl (in the neighboring Ukraine). Hundreds of thousands of people absorbed high doses of radiation. Around 20 percent of the farming land is still contaminated and unusable. Many villages remain abandoned.

A Grim Discovery

In June 1988, an archaeologist named Zianon Pazniak, the leader of a political party called the Christian Conservative Party of the Belarusian People's Front, discovered mass graves near the capital of Minsk. In them were about 250,000 bodies of victims executed in Belarus from 1937 to 1941. Many took this as proof that the Soviet government was trying to eliminate the Belarusian people altogether. As a result, Belarus began to seek independence.

Independence

The parliament of Belarus declared it a sovereign nation in 1990. Following the collapse of the Soviet Union, Belarus declared independence in 1991.

But the country can hardly be called free. President Alexander Lukashenko was elected in 1994, and he has ruled the country with an iron fist ever since. His policies have been so harsh that he is often viewed as Europe's last dictator. In 2005, during her testimony to the U.S. Congress, former U.S. Secretary of State Condoleeza Rice called Belarus Europe's only remaining "outpost of tyranny."

Belarus Today

Belarusians still do not have a strong sense of national identity. Those who oppose the government or its policies—even peacefully—face harsh penalties and imprisonment.

Lukashenko has prevented the privatization of state-run companies—which means the government continues to control businesses. As of 2005, there are virtually no private businesses in Belarus. As a result, investors from other countries cannot put money into Belarusian businesses, which would greatly strengthen the country's economy.

Although it has been discussed since 1999, a governmental and economic union that would unify Belarus and Russia into a single state still has not occurred. Belarus depends heavily on Russia for its oil and gas.

Lukashenko won a third term as president in 2006. There were widespread accusations among the citizens of vote-counting fraud. The government used extreme force on the demonstrators who gathered after the election to protest the result. The opposition presidential candidate was beaten, arrested, and sentenced to a five-year jail term. (He was released in 2008.)

Lukashenko will probably be president of Belarus for years to come. In 1996, he had the Belarus Constitution changed to allow him to remain in office for an unlimited amount of time after each election. The four state-run television stations and the government-controlled newspapers from which most people get their news will probably always support him. Much of the independent print media that opposes him has been forced to close down or publish in another country. Critics of the government are now turning to the Internet to express their views, doing such things as posting photos of opposition rallies to image-hosting web sites.

Relations between Belarus and the United States and Europe remain strained. The West continues to criticize Lukashenko's government for human rights violations against journalists, minorities, and anyone who opposes him. In the spring of 2008, Belarus withdrew its ambassador from Washington, DC. The following week, it asked U.S. Ambassador Karen Stewart to leave Belarus.

Belarus has released some of its political prisoners—which the United States and the European Union (EU) had been requesting for many years. But the country's relationship with the world remains strained. In 2009, Lukashenko did not accept the invitation of the EU to attend the Eastern Partnership Summit in Prague with six former Soviet states. Little news of Belarus ever reaches the greater world.

Daily Life

Most of the nearly 10 million people of Belarus live in the urban areas around the capital of Minsk and other major cities. There are people of more than 100 different nationalities in Belarus, including Russians, Poles, and Ukrainians. This multicultural population assures that the traditions of many cultures are blended into everyday life. Although people generally keep their political opinions to themselves (because of the political climate), they continue to enjoy life as much as possible.

Life in the Cities

The urban areas are the country's initial attractions to tourists. There is little crime in Belarus, so people are safe exploring the cities.

Many of the major cities are a feast for the eyes! Despite the great destruction of Belarus in World War II, many historic buildings have been restored.

Minsk is a thriving city with tidy streets, trendy stores, and lots of cafés and clubs where people enjoy getting together. There are beautiful forests at one end of the city. In 2008, construction workers in Minsk made an exciting discovery: the bones of two prehistoric mammoths between 25,000 and 45,000 years old!

Brest, which is in the southwest, on the border with Poland, is one of the country's most Westernized cities. It has beautiful parks, an ancient forest filled with bison, a National Center for Olympic Training in Rowing, a baseball stadium, and interesting landmark memorials.

Hrodna, in the west, is a center of Polish culture. It is known for its stunning variety of architecture, including Hrodna Castle.

Like Hrodna, Vitsebsk is known for its remarkable architecture, including one of the oldest buildings in the country: the Annunciation Church built in the 1140s.

In addition to the beautiful buildings, shops, and restaurants of Belarus, there are six national parks, a biosphere reserve north of Minsk, and many regional green spaces.

Life in Rural Areas

Rural life in Belarus contrasts greatly with city life. In fact, rural life is like a step back in time.

Many older rural homes are made of wood planks or logs, although you'll see newer brick homes, too. With both there is likely to be scrollwork around the doors, windows, and roofs. The ownership of homes in the country is passed down to each generation. There will probably be a well outside the home for water. There may also be an outdoor toilet.

Many people in rural areas are subsistence farmers who produce most of their own food. The entire family is involved in cutting wood, harvesting hay to feed livestock, and preserving fruits and vegetables. Some of the work, such as harvesting potatoes, may still be done with a horse-drawn plough.

Did You Know?

Belarus supplies 30 percent of the world's heavy-duty dump trucks.

Belarus supplies 10 percent of the world's tractors.

Most of the stores in Minsk are modern supermarkets.

There are about thirty types of bread made in Belarus.

Tadeusz Kościuszko (ta-deōs kos-chūs-kō) (1746–1817), a hero of the American Revolution who fought with and saved the life of George Washington, was a native of Belarus.

Belarus has the largest ancient forest in Europe.

Chaim (kīm) Wiezmann (1874–1952), who was born in Belarus, was a chemist who became the first president of Israel in 1949.

Home gardens are carefully maintained on small plots of land around the house and provide food and beautiful flowers. People pick mushrooms in the surrounding forests and might even sell them along the highway.

The fall harvest includes lots of apples! They'll be dried, canned, and pressed to make cider. Extra cash will come from selling them to large commercial processing plants. The farmers often put beehives among the apple trees to pollinate the apple blossoms in spring. They'll use the honey from these hives for cooking. Some of it will be sold in markets throughout Belarus.

Farm animals like chickens, ducks, turkeys, sheep, and goats round out the rural scene. Like the garden, these animals serve as important sources of food.

Getting Together with Family and Friends

Whether in the city or in the country, the people of Belarus are warm and friendly. They love to get together with family and friends.

The host will put out lots of food, sweets, and beverages, even for those visiting for just a short period of time. The host will also present bread and salt—two traditional symbols of hospitality—when greeting a guest. Visitors are expected to bring a small item, like a box of candy. People love to tell stories and share experiences.

Going to School

Basic education in Belarus is free. All children must attend primary and secondary schools from ages six to fifteen. They don't have to attend preschool, but about 70 percent of them do. After finishing this basic schooling and receiving a Certificate of Basic Education, students can start working or serve in the military. They can also attend college or professional technical institutions, where they can complete their high school education and work toward a professional certificate that allows them to continue on to university.

The academic year runs from September to July. Summer vacation runs through August.

Famous People from Belarus

Olga Korbut (1955–), who won gold medals in gymnastics at the 1972 and 1976 Olympic Games, is from Belarus.

Marc Chagall (1887–1985) was one of the most successful artists of the 20th century and was at the forefront of several art movements.

Louis Burt Mayer (1887–1957) was born in Minsk. Although he started out as a cinematographer, you know his name best as one of the founders of MGM (Metro-Goldwyn-Mayer) Studios in Hollywood.

Marc Chagall

Name _____ Date _____

PLAN A TRIP TO MINSK

Minsk is one of Europe's great capitals! Using the Internet and other resources to find information, plan a trip to Minsk. Answer these questions on another piece of paper.

1. Approximately how much will your round-trip ticket to Minsk cost?

2. You will need a passport if you don't already have one. How do you get a passport?

3. What is the name of the airport you will fly into?

4. Find a hotel in Minsk in which you would like to stay. What is the name of the hotel?

5. What special services does this hotel offer its guests (example: breakfast buffet, swimming pool)?

6. What public transportation will be available to you once you're in Minsk?

7. There are several museums in Minsk. Which two would you like to see? What type of art and artifacts would you see in each one?

8. Minsk is famous the world over for its architecture. Which two (or more) buildings would you like to see?

9. Minsk is filled with restaurants and cafés! Write the names of two you would like to visit.

10. What else would you like to do in Minsk?

Language & Expressions

Here are some fun facts about verbal and nonverbal communication in Belarus.

Body Language and Etiquette in Belarus

Here are some examples of body language and etiquette you'll find in Belarus.

Older people in Belarus will introduce themselves using their first name and patronymic (the name from their father). Use this full name when addressing them.

Belarusians are not usually emotional in public. If someone meets you with a hug and a kiss in public, you know the person likes you and considers you a friend.

Do not make the okay sign (creating a circle with the thumb and forefinger). Do not shake your fist. Both are considered rude.

Do not put your feet on the seat of a chair or table!

Don't whistle inside a building. It's considered bad luck.

Know before You Go

Here are some common phrases you will use in Belarus, along with the pronunciation. Try them out! Look up some additional ones!

English	Belarusian	Pronunciation
Hello.	Vitayu.	vit-āy-ū
Goodbye.	Da pabachen'nya.	da pab-ach-en-ya
Good morning.	Dobray ranitsy.	dō-brī ran-ēt-sē
Good evening.	Dobry vechar.	dō-brī vā-cher
Good night.	Dabranach.	da-bra-nach
Yes.	Tak.	tak
No.	Nye.	nī
Thank you.	Dziakuyu vam.	za-koy-u vam
You are welcome.	Nyama za shto.	nē-ama za shtō
What is your name?	Jak vas zavuts'?	yak vas za-voots
1	adzin	ad-zeen
2	dva	d-va
3	try	trī
4	chatyry	sha-tee-ree
5	piats'	pyats
6	shests'	shests
7	siem	syem
8	vosiem	vō-syem
9	dzieviats'	dzyev-yats
10	dziesiats'	dzees-yats

Foods

Simple, Hearty Cuisine

Belarusian cuisine is a blend of the cuisines of its neighboring countries, although the food is generally less complex and not as highly seasoned. It *is* hearty and savory, however—and there is a lot of it, at least at lunch and dinner. People typically start the day with a light breakfast and have a heavier lunch at mid-day. They save the biggest meal—a dinner served later in the evening—for last.

Common Foods

Most hot foods are slowly cooked or stewed. Simple recipes are handed down through generations. Heavier meals will usually include meat, potatoes, and wheat or rye bread.

The Ever-Popular Potato

Potatoes are called "the second bread" in Belarus—and with very good reason! Belarusians love potatoes so much that they have potato cafés throughout the country that feature special potato dishes.

You'll also find potatoes in salads and served with mushrooms and meats. Potato patties, baked potato puddings, and baked grated potato pies are common. Potato *draniki* (they're called *latkes* in North America) are thin pancakes made of shredded potatoes and eaten with sour cream. Belarusians eat lots of them!

Meat, Fish, and Side Dishes

Beef and pork are by far the most common meats eaten in Belarus. Salted pork fat is smoked and seasoned with onions and garlic. *Pyachysta*, a traditional holiday dish, is boiled, stewed, or roasted pig, chicken, or large chunks of pork or beef. Meat dishes are usually served with carrots, cabbage, black radishes, peas, mushrooms, and, of course, a potato dish. Many meat and vegetable dishes are prepared in stoneware pots and cooked for a long time. This is similar to the crock pot style of cooking in the United States. Fish dishes, such as trout, perch, and carp, are prepared with few spices, but they're still tasty!

Here are some favorite main dishes: sliced beef tongue with horseradish sauce; potato pancakes with meat in a mushroom sauce; meat roasted on a spit for barbeques; herring with potatoes; and pork stew.

Soups, Salads, and Sides

Soups are a favorite in Belarus at any time of year. Beetroot soup, bouillon, and cabbage soups are at the top of everyone's list. Cabbage and beetroot are found in salads, too, along with a special salad of tomatoes, cucumbers, and radishes.

Favorite side dishes include mushrooms served fresh, dried, salted, or pickled. Another popular side dish is *zacirka*. Pieces of dough are boiled in water and then served with milk poured over them and garnished with salted pork fat. (Milk is widely used in vegetable and flour dishes.) Cottage cheese and homemade yogurt appear on many Belarusian tables at all times of day.

Beverages

Kvass is a popular soft drink made from malted brown bread or rye flour. It's often flavored with fruits, like strawberries, or herbs like mint. It's also used in a cold summer soup with sliced vegetables called *okroshka*. Birch juice is a popular drink that has a delicate grape taste. (Yes, it's really from the birch tree!)

Desserts and Snacks

All sorts of berries (strawberries, raspberries, and cranberries) are eaten, mostly in their natural form. Apples are often baked. Ice cream with whipped cream is a dessert favorite.

Salted, roasted peanuts are a popular Belarusian snack, as are roasted chestnuts. You can get both from street vendors. As in America, boiled and salted corn on the cob is popular throughout the country. It's a common picnic food to take when visiting family in the country. Another snack is pickled eggs (sometimes dipped in beet juice to make them pink).

Holidays & Festivals

Holidays and Remembrance Days

Here are some holidays celebrated in Belarus.

New Year Day	January 1
Orthodox Christmas	January 7
International Women's Day	March 8
Constitution Day	March 15
Unity of the Peoples of Russia and Belarus Day	April 2
Catholic Easter	Movable Date
Orthodox Easter	Movable Date
Commemoration Day (Radonitsa)	ninth day after Orthodox Easter
Day of Remembrance of the Chernobyl Tragedy	April 26
Labor Day (Worker's Day)	May 1
Day of the National Emblem and Flag of Belarus	second Sunday in May
Victory Day	May 9
Independence Day (Day of the Republic)	July 3
October Revolution Day	November 7
Catholic Christmas	December 25

Women's Day • *March 8*

This holiday celebrates love and respect of women. Women receive gifts, flowers, and special good wishes—especially from the men in their lives.

Constitution Day • *March 15*

This marks the day (in 1994) when Belarus established its new Constitution.

Commemoration Day (Radonitsa) • *Ninth day after Orthodox Easter*

On this day, people visit cemeteries to lay flowers on the tombs of relatives and friends and pay their respects.

Unity of the Peoples of Russia and Belarus Day • *April 2*

On April 2, 1966, Alexander Lukashenko, President of Belarus, and Boris Yeltsin, former President of Russia, signed the Commonwealth Agreement of Belarus and Russia in Moscow. One year later, there was an agreement between the two countries to form a Belarus-Russia Union. This union has not yet occurred.

Labor Day (Worker's Day) • *May 1*

This is one of the most popular holidays in Belarus. It honors the nation's workers. People attend concerts and other public entertainment. Many families celebrate with picnics and barbecues.

Day of the National Emblem and Flag of Belarus • *Second Sunday in May*

This holiday honors the Belarusian emblem and flag, the main symbols of national unity and independence.

Victory Day • *May 9*

This day commemorates the victory in World War II, when 25 percent of the population of Belarus died. War veterans lead a large parade in Minsk Victory Square.

Independence Day • *July 3*

This special holiday marks the liberation of Minsk from the Nazi army by the Soviets in 1944. The occasion is marked by a large military parade in Minsk. People reflect on the fact that they won their country's freedom by suffering great losses.

Belarusian Written Language Day • *First Sunday in September*

First held in 1994, this major cultural holiday celebrates Belarusian literature and spiritual traditions. The holiday is traditionally held in a different city each year – one that has been a center of culture, science, literature, and book publishing. Festivities are also held throughout the country. Heads of government ministries, cultural workers, writers and poets, scientists, journalists, foreign embassy representatives, and international visitors all take part in the celebration. Festivities might include an exhibition of children's books, church services, concerts, and a closing ceremony to transfer a symbolic pennant to the next city to host the holiday.

Creative Arts

Belarus may be a relatively isolated country, but its creative arts are some of the finest in the world. All masterpieces of the arts—whether dance, music, theater performances, or art—are protected by the government. The government makes it easy for Belarusians to afford and have access to the many art exhibitions, performances, and festivals held all over the country each year. The government finances Belarusian art and cultural events inside and outside the country.

Music

Belarusians love music, and it is a part of their lives from the time they are young. Many people play at least one musical instrument. Music is sure to be a part of any holiday, festival, or party.

Belarusians love classical music and opera, and the country has three major symphony orchestras that include the Presidential Orchestra of the Republic of Belarus, the National Concert Orchestra of Belarus, and the State Academic Symphony Orchestra. Traditional folk music has a big following.

Since 2004, Belarus has been participating in the annual Eurovision Song Contest held among members of the European Broadcasting Union. Each member country submits a song to be performed on television. All the countries vote to determine the most popular song in the competition.

Belarus also hosts several music and cultural festivals that draw performers from all over the world. The annual Slavonic Bazaar in Vitebsk, an international festival of the arts, showcases Slavic music of Russia, Belarus, and the Ukraine.

Theater and Dance

Theater and dance are as much a part of daily life in Belarus as music. Children and adults alike enjoy puppet theaters in which fairy tales, folk tales, and other stories come to life through puppetry. Most of the larger cities in Belarus have their own puppet theater. Every major city also has an opera house, and many have professional theater companies.

Both kids and adults love to dance, and people take it seriously enough to study it throughout their lives. There are many excellent dance schools in Belarus that teach classical, folk, and contemporary dance. But ballet is the premier form of dance in Belarus, and every major city has a ballet company. Those who wish to pursue higher education in dance can attend the Belarusian National Ballet College or the Belarusian State Choreographic College. In 1996, the National Academic Theatre of Ballet in Minsk won the annual international ballet competition in Moscow and became the top ballet company in the world.

Fine Art

If you love fine art, you'll love Belarus! Its many museums house fine art in many styles and genres, from many time periods. The largest collection is in the National Art Museum of Belarus, in Minsk, where exhibits of the works of 17th to 21st century artists are featured and local artists also regularly exhibit their work.

After the October Revolution in Russia in 1917, the northern town of Vitebsk became the center for the avant-garde movement. Marc Chagall, one of the movement's best-known painters and one of the world's most famous artists, was born in Vitebsk in 1887. He founded the Vitebsk Arts College. He also organized the Vitebsk Museum of Modern Art in 1918 that contained paintings representing all of the movements in contemporary art worldwide. Although the museum was abolished in the mid-1920s, some of its paintings were transferred to the Vitebsk Regional Museum, which today houses thousands of paintings, artifacts, decorative arts, and even books and illustrations. The Chagall Art Center opened in 1997 in Vitebsk.

Traditional Dress

Traditional Belarusian dress resembles that of its neighboring countries, like Russia and Poland. It is generally only worn on festival days for celebrations. The clothing is usually made of flax or wool and is decorated with ornate patterns. Each region of Belarus has its own specific pattern. One pattern on some early costumes is currently used on the hoist side of the Belarusian national flag.

Sports Training for Everyone!

If you want to play sports for fun, train for competition, or catch a casual game, Belarus has what you're looking for! Belarusian kids—no matter how old they are—have access to some of the best sports facilities in Europe. There are hundreds of stadiums, swimming pools (even in kindergartens), athletic centers, ice rinks, and sports fields.

For top-notch training, the Raubichi Center in Minsk is one of the best biathlon centers in the world. It boasts miles of ski tracks and freestyle ski slopes, ski jumps, shooting grounds, gymnasiums, and swimming pools. At the Stayki Sports Complex, also in Minsk, athletes can train for Olympic competition in more than twenty sports. The country's other extensive training facilities include the Belarusian State University of Physical Education, colleges and special schools that train to Olympic standards, and more than 250 youth sports schools.

Favorite Sports and Games

Kids and adults alike in Belarus enjoy a broad range of sports. Among them are track and field, football (soccer), gymnastics, skiing, ice hockey, tennis, fencing, wrestling, volleyball, handball, and swimming. Favorite games include chess and checkers.

The Olympics

Belarus has taken part in the Olympic Games since 1952 as part of the Soviet Union's team. The country has an excellent Olympic record. The first independent Belarus team won two silver medals in the 1994 Winter Olympic Games. In the 2008 Beijing Games, it won nineteen medals, including four gold and five silver medals.

Belarus has also had a strong showing at the Paralympic Games, which are for athletes with physical and visual disabilities. At the 2008 Beijing Paralympics, Belarusian athletes won thirteen medals, including five gold medals.

"SHYLA"

Winter nights come early in Belarus. Kids play inside with their friends. This is one of the most popular winter games. It used to be played with an awl, a small tool called a *shyla* in Belarusian.

Number of Players Needed
Up to 20

Materials Needed
A tennis ball (or a small toy)

Directions
1. Choose a leader to start.
2. The leader stands in the center of the room.
3. The rest of the players sit down very close to each other in a half circle behind the leader's back. Their hands are behind their backs.
4. To begin, one of the players in the half-circle has the ball. He or she transfers it to someone else in the half-circle. This goes on until the leader calls "stop"!
5. Without looking at the players, the leader must guess who has the ball. If the leader is right, the person with the ball becomes the leader. The leader joins the semi-circle.

THE CZECH REPUBLIC

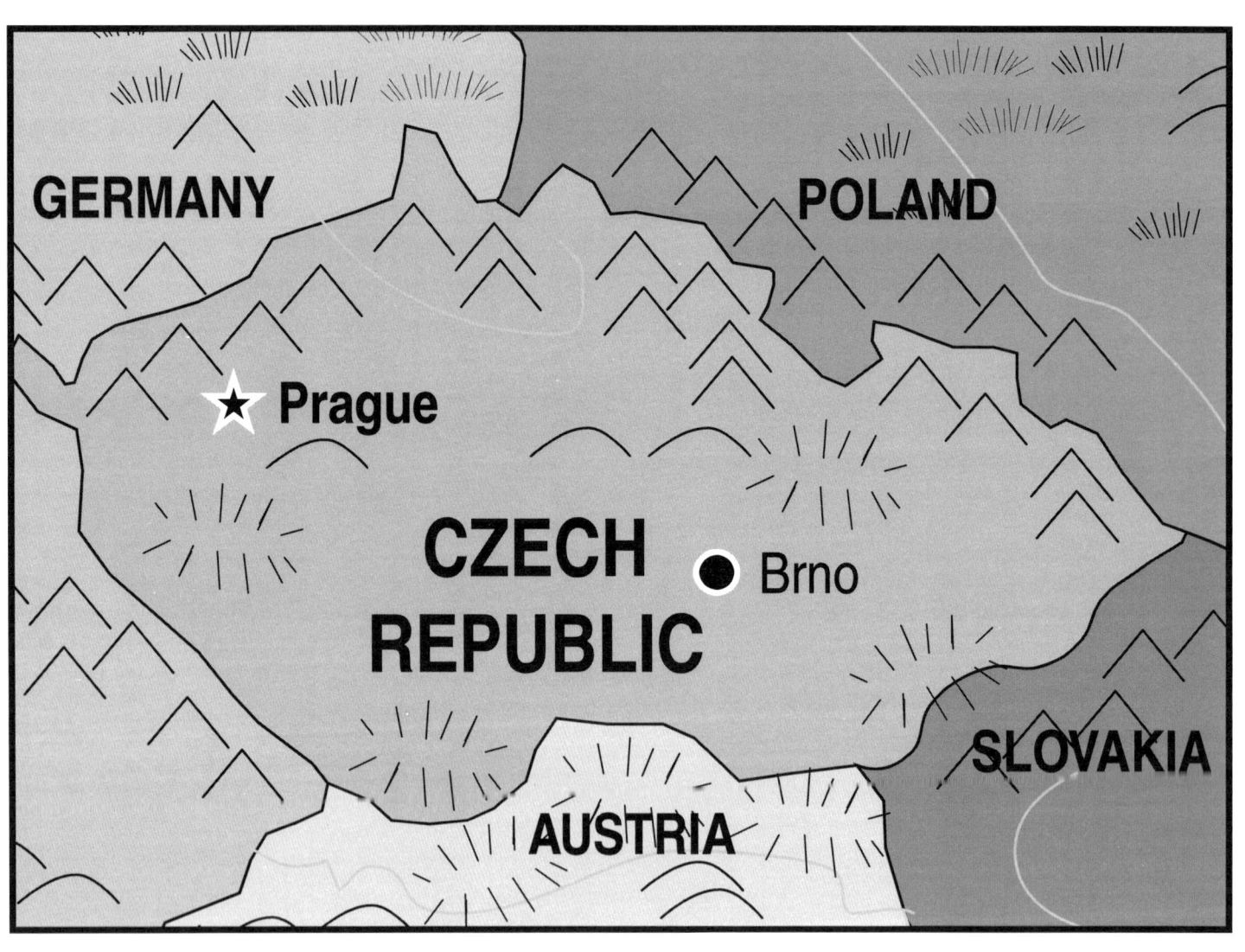

WELCOME TO THE CZECH REPUBLIC!

If you think the Czech (chek) Republic is still called Czechoslovakia, you're not alone. Although the Czech Republic and Slovakia officially separated in 1993, many in the Western world still don't know much about the Czech Republic. For starters, here's what you *should* know. It's now a democracy and no longer a Communist state. It's one of the most prosperous countries in Europe. With an economy on fast-forward, a rich culture, and more tourists discovering it each year, the Czech Republic is becoming a very high-profile global hot spot!

FAST FACTS

Official Name:	Czech Republic
Location:	Central Europe, between Germany, Poland, Slovakia, and Austria
Population:	10,201,707 (2010 estimate)
Capital City:	Prague
Area:	30,450 square miles. The Czech Republic is slightly smaller than the state of South Carolina.
Major Language:	Czech
Major Religions:	Roman Catholic: 26.8% Protestant: 2.1% Other: 3.3% Unspecified: 8.8% Unaffiliated: 59%
Currency:	Czech koruna (Czech crown) 1 koruna equals 100 haléřů (ha-lā-roo)
Climate:	Temperate; cool summers; cold, cloudy, humid winters
The Land:	In the west, Bohemia has plains, hills, and plateaus surrounded by low mountains. Moravia (in the east) is very hilly.
Type of Government:	Parliamentary democracy
Flag:	The Czech Republic flag is identical to the flag of the former Czechoslovakia. It has two equal horizontal bands of white (top) and red (bottom), with a blue isosceles triangle on the hoist side. The red and white colors are derived from the ancient Coat of Arms of Bohemia. The blue was added to differentiate it from the Polish flag.

MP5126 – Czech Republic

Coat of Arms:	The Coat of Arms displays the three historical regions that make up the Czech Republic. The arms of Bohemia show a silver double-tailed lion on a red background in the upper left and lower right-hand corners. The Moravian red-and-silver-checkered eagle is shown on a blue background in the upper right-hand corner. The arms of Silesia show a black eagle with a clover stalk on her breast on a golden background in the lower left-hand corner.
National Flower:	Rose
National Tree:	Linden
Motto:	"Truth prevails!"

Natural Environment

The landlocked Czech Republic has a beautiful natural environment of forests, hills, mountains, plains, and rivers. To the west is the region of Bohemia, which occupies about two-thirds of the country. It consists of a large, elevated basin drained by the Elbe and the Vltava (vul-tev-a) rivers. The basin is surrounded by low mountains, such as the Krkonoše (kār-kon-osh-ā) Range of the Sudetes Mountains. Sněžka, the highest point in the country, at 5,256 feet, is located there. Other mountain ranges that mark Bohemia's borders are the Bohemian Forest and the Ore Mountains. The mountain areas are famous for their ski resorts.

View from the summit of Sněžka

The Moravia region in the eastern part of the Czech Republic occupies about one-third of the country. It, too, is hilly. It is named for the Moravian River, which flows in northwest Moravia. Moravia is also the source of the Oder River.

Plants and Animals

The forests, fields, and wetlands of the Czech Republic are teeming with many of the common species of animals living in the wild in Europe. This includes rabbits, otters, pheasants, partridges, wild boars, red deer, waterfowl (such as ducks and geese), eagles, and herons. In northeastern Moravia, there are wolves and brown bears.

About two-thirds of the indigenous forests in the Czech Republic (those that have been there for centuries) are made up of spruce trees. The rest of the forests contain a mixture of oak, fir, and spruce. The national tree of the Czech Republic is the linden. In fact, the largest living tree in the country is a linden located in Moravia. The perimeter of the trunk is about 41 feet!

A History of the Czech Republic

Arrival of the Slavic Tribes

Historians have not pinpointed the exact date when the Czech lands came to be occupied. They think that around the fifth century CE, Slavic tribes from modern-day Poland settled in Bohemia, Moravia, and Silesia. (Silesia is a region now mostly in Poland with parts in the northeastern and eastern Czech Republic and eastern Germany.)

The Czech Lands

The Great Moravian Empire

The first state in the Czech lands was the Great Moravian Empire, located in the territories of Bohemia, Silesia, Moravia, Slovakia, and the Danube River Basin. It was bordered by the powerful East Frankish Kingdom, which was Christian. As a result, Christianity spread to Moravia. Slavic missionaries arrived, and Moravia eventually became a bishopric of the Church. The Great Moravian Empire ended around the 10th century with invasion of the Magyars in the middle Danube area. After this, the power of the state moved west to the Kingdom of Bohemia.

The Kingdom of Bohemia

Bohemia became a powerful region in the Middle Ages and remained part of the Holy Roman Empire until 1806. (The Holy Roman Empire was a union of central European territories under a Holy Roman Emperor.) The Přemyslid Czech royal dynasty ruled the Kingdom of Bohemia, which included Moravia and Silesia, from the 10th to the 16th centuries.

During the Middle Ages, many people from Germany migrated east to Bohemia. The Germans populated towns and districts along the Bohemian border and created colonies further inland.

The Přemyslid line died out in 1306. After a series of wars, the House of Luxembourg gained the Bohemian crown. This began what is called the Golden Age of Czech history—particularly during the reign of Charles IV (1346–1378). Charles made Prague the imperial capital. It remains the capital of the Czech Republic today. He founded Charles University in Prague in 1347. Still in existence, it is the oldest and largest university in the Czech Republic and one of the oldest in Europe. He built the Charles Bridge that crosses the Vlata River in Prague. He also funded St. Vitus Cathedral in Prague, which is still the biggest and most important church in the Czech Republic.

Unfortunately, the Black Plague, one of the deadliest diseases ever known, began to sweep across Europe in 1347. By 1380, much of the population of Bohemia had died.

Jan Hus

In the 15th century, Jan Huss (1369–1415), a Catholic priest and teacher at Charles University, began a movement to reform the Catholic Church in Bohemia. Hus did not like some of the church's practices, and his teaching had a strong influence on many in Europe who agreed with him. They particularly influenced Martin Luther, the German priest who broke from the Catholic Church and founded the Lutheran Church a century later. Nevertheless, the Catholic Church considered Huss a heretic. He was burned at the stake in 1415.

His followers broke from the Catholic Church. In the Hussite Wars from 1419 to 1434, they defeated five military crusades organized against them by the Holy Roman Emperor. The Czech Hussite Reformation movement continued for the next 200 years. About 90 percent of the people in Bohemia converted to Hussite Protestantism.

July 6, the anniversary of the execution of Jan Huss, is a public holiday in the Czech Republic. He is considered a martyr and a national hero. The Czechoslovak Hussite church still exists in the Czech Republic.

The House of Habsburg

Ferdinand I, of the House of Habsburg, became King of Bohemia in 1526. Bohemia came under Habsburg rule, but the Czechs rebelled against it, starting in 1618. This began the Thirty Years' War (1618–1648) that eventually spread to Germany. The war was one of the deadliest in European history. The Czechs' rebellion in Bohemia was crushed in 1620, and the country became part of the Austrian Empire for the next 300 years. The people were not free of the Habsburgs until the end of World War I, when the Austrian-Hungarian Empire collapsed.

Czechs call the period from 1620 to the late 18th century the Dark Age because the Thirty Years' War devastated their lands. The Habsburgs banned all religions but Catholicism. The thousands of Czech Protestants who refused to convert were banished from the country. War and famine killed thousands more. In the end, about one-third of the population of Bohemia was lost. Later, in 1663, the Ottoman Turks and Tatars invaded Moravia in the east and took 12,000 people as slaves.

Maria Theresa of Austria (1740–1780) and her son Joseph II (1780–1790) ruled the Czech lands as Holy Roman Emperor and co-regent from 1765. Their reigns were noted for tolerance of religion, promotion of the arts and sciences, and reforms in education. In 1742, King Frederick II of Prussia seized most of Silesia, which was then under the Habsburgs. This began the eight-year War of the Austrian Succession, a struggle between the Habsburgs and Prussia for the region of Silesia. Ultimately, Prussia won control of Silesia.

After the fall of the Holy Roman Empire in 1806, the Kingdom of Bohemia became part of the Austrian Empire. In 1867, it became part of Austria–Hungary. After the Revolution of 1848, Emperor Franz Josef I of Austria attempted to rule as the absolute king of all the nationalities in the Kingdom of Bohemia.

The Republic of Czechoslovakia

World War I

In 1918, following the collapse of the Austro-Hungarian Empire after World War I, the Czech lands and Slovakia were joined to become the independent republic of Czechoslovakia.

The newly formed country gave extensive rights to the great number of minority groups living in the land, including Germans, Hungarians, and Poles. But it did not grant them the right to govern their own territories. Failing to do this resulted in some minorities wanting to break with Czechoslovakia.

World War II

In 1939, Nazi troops occupied the country. Adolf Hitler, the German dictator, made Bohemia and Moravia protectorates of Nazi Germany. They remained so until the end of the War. As they did in other countries, the Nazis devastated Czechoslovakia and its people. Of the approximately 120,000 Jews in the country, 80,000 were killed.

The former Czech government returned to the country in 1945, after the war ended. But the hatred that the Czechoslovakians had for the Germans spilled over into the Czechs' treatment of its German minorities. In the months after World War II, the Czech government expelled many Germans living in Czechoslovakia.

The Communist State of Czechoslovakia

The Communist Party won the elections of 1946 and became the dominant political party. In 1948, a group of ministers from the existing Czech political parties resigned to protest the Communists gaining control. The Communists seized power, saying they had to reconstruct the government. In the elections that followed, only Communist Party candidates were on the ballot. Thus, the Communists gained complete control of the Czechoslovakian government in 1948. The Czechoslovakian democracy became a Communist state.

As in other former Soviet bloc countries, Communist rule was brutal and oppressive. The Communists either put their political opponents to death or put them in concentration camps. A so-called "Iron Curtain" separated Czechoslovakia from the free world. It became a nation the world knew little about.

In August of 1968, forces from the Soviet Union and other countries invaded Czechoslovakia to stop its leader, Alexander Dubček, an effort he called "Prague Spring." This was Dubček's attempt to reform the Communist government, free political prisoners, and restore basic human rights in Czechoslovakia. The invasion crushed Dubček's reform efforts. The Communists remained in power for another 21 years and continued to imprison and persecute those who opposed the regime.

Velvet Revolution

The Communist rule ended in 1989 with an astonishingly bloodless overthrow of the Communists called the "Velvet Revolution." Václav Havel was elected president. Havel was a playwright; the Communists had imprisoned him twice and banned his plays. The world rallied around him as a symbol for human rights. Democracy returned to Czechoslovakia.

The Czech Republic

With the return of democracy, the Slovakian people sought independence. They got it in 1993 with the "Velvet Divorce," in which Czechoslovakia split into the Czech and Slovak republics. The Czech Republic joined NATO in March 1999. It is now also a member of the United Nations, and its armies have participated in missions to Iraq, Afghanistan, and many other countries. Havel continued to lead the Czech Republic until 2003. He is still seen as an international figure of courage and hope.

The Country Today

In May 2004, the Czech Republic joined the European Union. Today, it is a democracy with a growing economy, thanks in great part to its EU membership. Living standards are approaching those of other EU countries. People can now own their own property. Lifestyles are becoming more Westernized, but centuries-old traditions are honored and maintained.

Moreover, the world is discovering the Czech Republic! The country annually greets visitors from all over the globe. The country is actively seeking immigrants from other countries, billing itself as a promising young country in Europe. The Iron Curtain that once hid this beautiful, historic land from the greater world has finally been lifted.

Daily Life

The Family Unit

Whether living in a bustling city or a rural hamlet, Czechs enjoy and rely on their families for support throughout their lives. Two or three generations may live together under one roof. Grandparents and other extended family members help with the babysitting and household chores. Parents stay involved with their kids well after the kids have moved out on their own.

Family roles are fairly traditional. A father is usually the head of the family; a mother exercises much more authority over the kids. New mothers who have jobs outside the home can get up to three years of maternity leave with a percentage of their full pay! (Compare this to the six or eight weeks of maternity leave that mothers in America usually get.) This allows a mother to stay at home during a child's first couple of years if she chooses to do so.

Czech children are expected to be obedient, hardworking, and respectful at home, at school, and in public.

Czech Homes

In larger cities, such as Prague, many people live in apartments (called *flats*) and housing developments. The apartments are small by American standards. The bedrooms will probably not have closets, so people use wardrobes, chests, and dressers for storage. Family houses, particularly in urban and suburban areas, are built of concrete block or brick rather than wood. The incredible contrast between old and new is illustrated in many larger Czech cities, where drab apartment buildings and housing blocks sit next to beautiful Old Town areas, with castles or churches that date back several centuries.

Prague

Things are a little different in the countryside, where parents commonly live with their grown kids. Houses are much more common and are more likely to be constructed of wood. People who own homes in rural areas often build them with rooms for their parents, too.

Weekends and Free Time

Unlike those who go into the office for a few hours or take work home for the weekend, Czechs do not work on Saturday and Sunday. People use these days to rest and recharge. City folks often head for their country cottages.

The weekend starts on Friday afternoon. Shops close early, and work life winds down. Those who don't go to a cottage head for parks and other recreation areas to bicycle, hike, roller-blade, ski, or walk the dog. Or they head to a local restaurant or café for coffee, conversation, and maybe some Internet surfing. There are lots of Wi-Fi hot spots all over the Czech Republic. In fact, the country has the most Wi-Fi subscribers of any country in the European Union.

Music figures heavily into free time as well. Many children take music lessons when they're young. Many adults still play an instrument. Whatever age, the popular saying "All Czechs are musicians" applies!

Are We There Yet?

The public transportation system in the Czech Republic is excellent. Getting around is easy.

The local city bus lines are well-run, clean, modern, and run on schedule. Some of the bus lines link the larger cities. Automated voices on the buses call out the stops. Many of the buses are double-length with a bend in the middle. You buy your tickets from a kiosk next to the bus stop. You can also buy them from the driver, but they're more expensive if you do.

The country makes it easy for bicyclists to enjoy the ride. Hundreds of people bicycle in the cities especially since it's much easier to maneuver in traffic on a bike. The country roads have paths marked for cyclists. If you get tired while bicycling out in the country, it's easy to find a train back home and store your bicycle in the baggage section.

The metro (subway) system and trams (streetcars) are also great ways to get around in the larger cities. It's still tough to get around in a car—until you get outside the city, though you need a toll sticker to drive on the motorways.

The train system in the Czech Republic goes to even the most remote locations in the country. There are several types of trains. Some connect the cities to the suburbs. Some stop at every station. Some skip small villages and stop at towns only. Some only run between the major cities. Everybody uses the trains, and they're generally safe and inexpensive. They're not considered modern, however! The country is still working on upgrading their Communist-era railways.

Shopping

There are some large department stores in the Czech Republic, and more are certainly on the way. Big shopping centers are being built in and around the larger cities. Today, you'll find well-known chains like the Swedish firms IKEA® and H&M®, along with the British firm Marks & Spencer®.

This is still a land of small specialty shops, however. These include butcher shops, bakeries, fruit and vegetable stores, and candy shops. Not only do they contain delicious things, they look the part of small charming shops in a beautiful European setting.

Going to School

Many Czech children go to day nurseries around age three and to kindergarten around age five. All kids go to school from ages six to 15. They attend elementary school for the first five years. After that, they have a few options. Those who want to go to university move to an eight-year secondary school called a *gymnasium*. They must pass written exams to get in and take final exams when they leave.

Another option is to take nine years of basic education. After that, students can take the last four years of gymnasium or go to a special four-year school that prepares them for vocational positions such as nurse or electrician.

Public kindergartens and primary and secondary schools are free. There are some private and parochial (religious) schools, but many parents cannot afford the tuition. University is free, but students must pay for their books, room, and board.

Famous Czechs

Sports, the arts, science, psychology—so many well-known people who have made great contributions to these fields are from the Czech Republic or the former Czechoslovakia. Here are a few from a very long list!

Martina Navrátilová (1956–) is one of the most famous Czechs—and tennis players—the world has ever known! She has won twenty Wimbledon titles and a total of 59 Grand Slams (the most important tennis events of the year). She was also proclaimed World's Best Player in 1978–1979 and 1982–1986, as well as World's Best Sportswoman in 1983–1984.

Ivan Lendl (1960–) is a former World #1 tennis player. During the 1980s and early 1990s, he was one of the world's biggest tennis stars. He won 94 tournaments, including eight Grand Slams.

Czech film director Miloš Forman (1932–) is famous for *One Flew over the Cuckoo's Nest* (1975) and *Amadeus* (1984), considered two of the best films in American cinema. He won the Academy Award as Best Director for both.

Sigmund Freud (1836–1930) was born in Moravia, Austria-Hungary, which is now the Czech Republic. Even if you don't know much about Freud, you'll often hear his name. He developed psychotherapy (what we today call therapy or counseling) to treat mental illness or mental distress. His ideas and work continue to influence many people.

Antonín Dvořák (1841–1904) is one of the world's most famous composers. Many of his operas, symphonies, and other music incorporate the melodies of folk music from Moravia and Bohemia. His most famous work is the *New World Symphony*.

Franz Kafka (1883–1924) was one of the world's great authors. Much of his work is considered to be among the most important in world literature. He's most famous for the short story *Metamorphosis* and a novel entitled *The Trial*.

Sigmund Freud

Language & Expressions

Here are some fun facts about verbal and nonverbal communication in the Czech Republic.

Famous Czech Proverbs

Here are ten famous Czech proverbs. What do you think they mean?

A habit is a shirt made of iron.
The way you eat is the way you work.
The way to be safe is never to feel secure.
If you buy things you don't need, you are stealing from yourself.
Hope is a great breakfast but a poor dinner.
There are no cakes without work.
Cleanliness is half your health.
He who digs a pit for another falls into it himself.
Even small fish are fish.
You will get furthest with honesty.

Body Language and Etiquette in the Czech Republic

Here are some examples of body language and etiquette you'll find in the Czech Republic.

What you wear on your feet—and where you wear it—is important in the Czech Republic. Most Czechs wear slippers or "house shoes" in the house. Outdoor shoes like boots and sandals are for outdoor wear only. When visiting, leave your shoes at the door. Your host may even have slippers for you.

Many Czechs don't have carpeted floors, and they don't sit on bare floors. This is considered an invitation to get a cold from the draft.

It may take years of constant contact with someone before you address the person by first name. Generally, family members and very good friends address each other by first name. They address everyone else by their title, such as Mr., Mrs., Miss, and Dr.

Only good friends get invitations to a Czech apartment. This is because the small apartments don't have room for a lot of people.

Czechs stand an arm's length away from each other in conversation.

Czechs generally do not make a special point of talking while they're dining.

Know before You Go

Here are some common phrases you will use in the Czech Republic. The spelling and pronunciation are also given. Try them out! Look up some additional ones!

English	Czech	Pronunciation
Hello. Goodbye.	Ahoj.	AH'hoy.
Thank you.	Děkuji.	DICK-keww.
You're welcome.	Prosim.	PRO-seem.
I'm sorry.	Promiňte.	PROM-min-the.
Excuse me.	S dovolením.	Zd'-ovo-le-nee.
Yes.	Ano.	AH'noh.
No.	Ne.	Neh.
My name is….	Jmenuji se …	Y'me-noo-yi se.
What is your name?	Jak se jmenujete?	YAK se y'me-noo-ye-te?
Where is…?	Kde je …?	Gday yeh…?

Name _____   Date _____

CZECH IDIOMS

An idiom is an expression that has a different meaning from the actual individual words themselves.

Example: I'm **sitting on the fence** about whether or not to go to the game.
Meaning: I don't know whether or not to go to the game.

Most languages have idioms. Some Czech idioms mean the same thing as Western idioms. Rewrite each sentence below, and substitute a common idiom for the Czech idiom in bold. The first one has been done for you.

1. The speaker took a long time to get to the **core of the issue**.
   *The speaker took a long time to get to the **heart of the matter**.*

2. Buying things you don't need is just like **throwing money out the window**.
   _____

3. The speaker had a **dumpling in her throat**.
   _____

4. If I get to the store and the post office before noon, I **kill two flies with one hit**.
   _____

5. The argument they got into was just a **storm in a glass of water**.
   _____

6. I looked outside, and it was **raining as if from a watering can**.
   _____

7. Miguel knows Martin **like he knows his own shoes**.
   _____

8. I'll **hold my thumbs** that your team wins the game!
   _____

9. Before James went onstage, his classmate whispered, **"Break a neck!"** for good luck.
   _____

10. Angelo **walked around hot porridge** instead of getting to the point.
    _____

Daily Meals

Czechs eat their main meal of the day at noon, and it's usually the type of hot, three-course meal (soup, main dish, and dessert) that most Westerners would eat in the evening. Dinner, which is later in the evening, is more like British tea. It usually includes a hot beverage and finger foods like doughnuts or rolls to get you through the evening. It generally wouldn't even include sandwiches or side dishes.

The Czech diet includes a great deal of meat, potatoes and other starches, butter, cream, sugar, fat, and sauces. But since Czechs get so much physical exercise walking, bicycling, or running for the bus during the week, it's no wonder Czechs stay healthy.

People eat more elaborate meals on the weekends than they do Monday through Friday. A typical Sunday or special occasion dinner might include roast beef served with a rich sour-cream sauce, roast duck, or goose—all of which would be served with dumplings and sauerkraut. No delicious Czech meal will begin without everyone saying, *"Dobrou Chut!"* This means "Hope it tastes good!"

Common Foods

Meats, Fish, and Side Dishes

Common meals include a great deal of pork, along with beef and chicken. Organ meats, such as liver, kidney, and brain, are also common. Many meats are prepared with gravy and filling side dishes, like potatoes (roasted, mashed, or boiled) and dumplings. Other side dishes are French fries, rice, or potato salad.

Fish is not as common as meat. Trout, cod, salmon, and mackerel are sometimes served, especially in restaurants. Carp is a traditional dish on Christmas Eve.

Soups

Popular soups are chicken or beef soup with liver dumplings, potato soup with mushrooms, garlic soup, chicken noodle soup, sauerkraut soup, and dill soup made with sour milk. One favorite you may have to develop a taste for if you visit the country is potato and tripe soup (tripe is the lining of a cow's stomach). People often eat croutons in their soup or carve a thick slice of bread to go with it.

Vegetables

Potatoes, carrots, peas, onions, peppers, tomatoes, and cabbage are the most common vegetables used in just about every hot dish from soups to roasts. Raw cabbage is served as a side with everything! Sometimes vegetables are made into delicious sauces to spread over meat dishes. Salads (as we think of them—lettuce with veggies and a dressing) are not as common in the Czech Republic.

Mushrooms deserve a special mention. Mushroom picking is a popular pastime in the Czech Republic. There are hundreds of species, and some are actually deadly. Kids are taught from their earliest years to distinguish poisonous from nonpoisonous varieties. It's not at all unusual to see a family on a weekend afternoon, pails in hand, picking their favorites. At home, they make them into an incredible variety of dishes, including mushroom caps dipped in breadcrumbs and fried, stewed mushrooms, mushroom sauce served with meat and dumplings, and creamy mushroom and potato soup.

Sweets and Desserts

It's practically a law in Eastern Europe: Everyone loves sweets! Czechs are no exception. Their sweets and desserts are delicious, and they often include doughy crusts with fruit or cheese fillings. Sweets are so important that the *cukrárna* (a shop that sells sweets and ice cream) is often the one place open on Sunday in the villages and small towns.

Fruit dumplings are at the top of the Czech dessert list. Commonly made with plums or apricots, they're served with grated cheese and browned bread crumbs sprinkled with sugar. People sometimes eat these as a meal.

Buchty are rectangular yeast buns filled with jam or preserves. *Koláče* (kol-a-che) are small cakes with a filling of poppy seeds, plum jam, or sweetened farmer cheese. (Farmer cheese is similar to cottage cheese, but it's drier and firmer.) *Bábovka* is a semi-sweet cake baked in a ring. Pancakes are popular, too! Thin pancakes are spread with jam, rolled up, and dusted with powdered sugar. Other desserts include lots of different cream cakes, warm apple strudel with whipped cream, gingerbread cake with honey and walnuts—the list could go on and on!

Koláče

Holidays & Festivals

Many Czech public holidays (apart from Christmas and Easter) honor various national heroes and significant events in the life of the country. There are usually radio and TV programs to commemorate many of these special days. But most people will spend them enjoying a day off with friends and family, and going to special events, like games and concerts.

Easter and Easter Monday • *March or April*

Before the Czech Republic became a free country again, the Communists didn't allow people to celebrate the religious holiday of Easter. Easter is now celebrated over two days, with many traditions and customs related to spring and new beginnings.

As with all Eastern European countries, the hand-decorated Easter egg is a primary symbol of this holiday. In the Czech Republic, girls decorate eggs to be given to boys on Easter Monday. Prague and other Czech cities hold Easter egg decorating contests.

The customary dinner on Easter is lamb. Getting together with family and friends is the hallmark of this day.

On Easter Monday, it's customary for guys to tap girls on the legs with a wicker stick or willow twig with colorful streamers tied to the end of it. Health and happiness is said to come to anyone tapped with the twig. The guys hope the women will give them colored eggs or candy in return. At noon, the girls pour water on the guys!

Labor Day • *May 1*

This public holiday honors the nation's workers.

Liberation Day • *May 8*

This holiday commemorates the day (in 1945) when the Germans signed an unconditional surrender and ended World War II in Europe.

Last Ringing • *(Late April or Early May)*

This is a fun celebration day for students leaving high school, and takes place just before they take their final exams. Kids get a day off school and do silly things like collecting money from passersby, wearing costumes, or spraying people with perfume. They use any money they collect for a party after exams.

Saints Cyril and Methodius Day • *July 5*

This day honors the great Slavic missionaries St. Cyril and St. Methodius. They came to Moravia in 863 to spread the Christian faith.

Jan Hus Day • *July 6*

People remember Jan Hus, the great religious reformer who was burned at the stake in 1415 for his views. The Czech people honor him as a martyr and a national hero.

St. Wenceslas Day (Czech Statehood Day) • *September 28*

St. Wenceslas (wen-sus-les) is the same person in the famous Christmas carol "Good King Wenceslas." He is the patron saint of the Czech Republic, known for his good works and kindness to all. This feast day honors the death of Wenceslas who was murdered by his brother in 935 CE. Wenceslas was made a saint after he died. He is said to have worked many miracles after his death.

Independent Czechoslovak State Day (Czech Founding Day) • *October 28*

This day marks the founding of Czechoslovakia in 1918.

Struggle for Freedom and Democracy Day • *November 17*

This is a day for reflection, remembrance, and celebration. It commemorates the student demonstrations against Nazi occupation in 1939, as well as the demonstration in 1989 that started the Velvet Revolution.

The Christmas Season

Christmas is the premier celebration season in the Czech Republic. People start buying gifts and baking supplies well before December. When December comes, the month starts off with a week's worth of housecleaning to prepare for the festivities. This is the time of year when people get together often, forgive each other, and feast! Many days of the month have special celebrations.

St. Barbara's Day (December 4)

On this day, people put a cherry tree branch in water in a warm place like the kitchen. The branch blooms during the Christmas season—a sign of good luck. If the girl who tends the branch is of marriageable age, she will marry a good man within one year—*if* the branch blooms on Christmas Eve.

St. Nicholas Day (December 6)

This day officially kicks off the holiday season with the baking of Christmas goodies. It's called the Feast of Svaty Mikulaš (St. Nicholas or Santa Claus). Svaty Mikulaš—like Santa Claus—keeps track of good and bad children! He walks around the village in a red robe with an angel who carries a big book and a devil who rattles chains. He asks children if they've been good during the year. The angel records their responses. That evening, the good kids will get candy, nuts, fruit, and small gifts in their shoes. The bad kids can expect a lump of coal, potatoes, or rocks!

Christmas Eve (December 24)

Christmas Eve in the Czech Republic is the day when people celebrate Christmas. The family decorates the Christmas tree in the afternoon with natural ornaments like apples, walnuts, and gingerbread. Though Czechs don't eat much fish during the year, it's traditional to have an evening meal of fried carp or carp soup, usually accompanied by potato salad and a whole lot of sweet goodies.

Since St. Nick has already visited, tradition has it that the baby Jesus has placed the gifts under the Christmas tree. The presents are opened on the evening of the 24th. After that, people attend a midnight church service filled with music, candles, and best wishes for a happy holiday.

Christmas Day (December 25)

The family goes to church and eats a big meal at noon. There is traditionally so much food at this meal that people eat only once on Christmas. This is a traditional day for visiting friends and relatives.

St. Stephen's Day (December 26)

The entire country takes the day off. Kids go caroling for treats. Families go for walks together or continue visiting friends and relatives. Everyone rests from the intense holiday activities.

New Year's Eve (December 31)

People celebrate much the same way everyone in the world celebrates—with a party that usually goes long into the night. There's lots of food, music, dancing, and wishing each other good luck for the coming year.

New Year's Day and Restoration Day of the Independent Czech State (January 1)

In addition to welcoming the New Year, people remember this as the date the Czech Republic was created in 1993 after the dissolution of Czechoslovakia.

Three Kings Day (January 6)

Young boys dress up as kings and go caroling in the neighborhood for treats.

Name _____ Date _____

YOUR FAVORITE HOLIDAY

You've just read about the special foods and traditions of Czech holidays. Choose one of your favorite holidays or family celebrations, like a birthday or name day.

Think about the things you do to prepare for this special day and the way you actually celebrate it. Answer the questions below. Then share your answers with your classmates. Consider bringing in a favorite song or anything else that best represents this day to share with your classmates!

1. Name of the holiday _____
   _____

2. Date or dates the holiday is celebrated _____
   _____

3. Purpose of the holiday _____
   _____

4. History of the holiday _____
   _____

5. Colors associated with the holiday _____
   _____

6. Special symbols associated with the holiday _____
   _____

7. Special foods associated with this holiday _____
   _____

8. How you and your family prepare for this holiday _____
   _____

9. How you and your family traditionally spend the day _____
   _____

10. What you especially like about this holiday and look forward to each year _____
    _____

Czech Republic – MP5126

Creative Arts

Music

Music is by far the most popular creative art in the Czech Republic, and it has been for centuries. Although not many Czechs choose to become professional musicians, they will likely love music all of their lives and play an instrument. The old saying that "Every Czech is a musician" is not an exaggeration!

While operas and symphonies dominated prior centuries, jazz, bluegrass, and pop are as popular here as they are in Western countries. Every May, music lovers from all over the world attend the Prague Spring International Music Festival. It features some of the world's best performing artists, symphony orchestras, and chamber music ensembles.

Puppet Theaters

The Czech Republic has a long tradition of puppetry. The use of puppets—particularly marionettes—goes back to the 12th century, when they were a key element in religious ceremonies and folk festivals. By the 16th century, performers from Austria and Germany began doing puppet shows in the Czech markets. A century later, Italian performers and their puppets did the same. By the mid-18th century, Czechs were learning puppetry from these wandering performers, handing down puppets and scripts through the generations.

By the time Czechoslovakia had become a country in 1918, there were many puppet theaters and puppetry associations throughout the country, performing for adults and children alike. During World War II, when the Nazis forbade puppetry, some puppeteers put on "underground" performances to show their opposition to the Nazis.

Today, puppetry is as popular as ever. Walk down any street in a major city like Prague, and you'll likely find marionettes performing for the tourists. A professional network of puppet theaters in the Czech Republic puts on performances ranging from operas to fairy tales. Prague's Rise Loutek Theater is home to the National Marionette Theater.

Laterna Magika

Laterna magika (Magic Lantern), found in Prague, is an unusual theatrical experience that has been drawing people from all over the world for fifty years. The plays and performances combine live theater, film, dance, music, and lights to create multimedia productions that are easy to follow no matter what language you speak. The production company has appeared all over the world. Laterna Magika has made Czech theater internationally famous.

Architecture

The Czech Republic is famous for its architecture. There are 12 UNESCO World Heritage Sites around the country. Gothic castles, medieval stone churches, chateaus, fortresses and forts, modern Cubist-style buildings—you'll see all kinds of architecture. Much of it is remarkably well preserved and open to the public. Some castles serve as elegant backdrops for cultural events like music festivals, theatrical performances, and even national chess exhibitions. Some castles even have their own zoos of exotic animals, not to mention collections of fine art and artifacts.

The capital of Prague alone has thousands of buildings of many artistic styles, as well as fortified settlements around the city that developed toward the end of the ninth century. The skyline is filled with all types of architecture. Buildings to visit in Prague include the Old Prague City Hall with its famous astronomical clock and the U.S. Embassy in the remodeled 17th century Schoenborn Palace. You'll find lots of other buildings to capture your interest, too!

The "Dancing House"

Prague Castle

Name _____   Date _____

FAMOUS CASTLES OF THE CZECH REPUBLIC

There are hundreds of castles in the Czech Republic. Here are twelve of them. Find them in the word search below. They can be listed across, up, down, or backwards.

K	D	Z	C	E	V	O	K	A	R	K
A	E	K	U	N	E	T	I	C	K	A
M	T	D	E	N	N	S	Z	W	A	R
E	S	M	A	R	R	I	P	O	U	L
N	I	R	O	K	O	K	V	V	V	S
N	P	O	U	N	V	O	K	O	S	T
P	O	R	E	P	O	R	S	I	O	E
R	N	E	S	Q	W	L	X	Z	Z	J
L	O	T	O	C	N	I	K	L	P	N
P	K	R	I	V	O	K	L	A	T	S
O	A	O	P	E	X	F	I	T	T	T
W	J	S	X	G	V	O	K	I	V	Z
R	Z	K	L	H	P	L	E	O	O	R
T	B	Y	P	W	D	E	P	D	A	A

KAMEN   KRIVOKLAT
KARLSTEJN   KUNETICKA
KOKORIN   ORLIK
KONOPISTE   TOCNIK
KOST   TROSKY
KRAKOVEC   ZVIKOV

Karlstejn Castle

Sports & Games

Sports

The Soviets emphasized excellence in sports. Playing sports continues to be a popular pastime in the Czech Republic. There are hundreds of relatively new and well-maintained athletic facilities for swimming, ice hockey, tennis, football (soccer), and basketball.

Downhill and cross-country skiing and snowboarding are the most popular winter sports. Beach areas draw thousands each summer for swimming, diving, and sunbathing. Hiking is popular no matter the time of year. Extreme sports fans will find places set up for bungee jumping and rock climbing.

Ice Hockey and Football

Czechs support their national sports as avidly as any fans in the world. Tickets for in-country league games are inexpensive, and fans flock to the arenas.

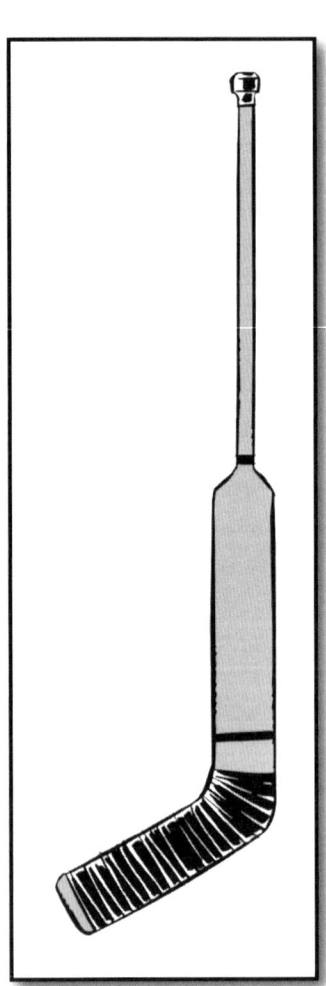

The Czech National Hockey team is one of the top-rated in the world and won its first gold medal at the 1998 Nagano Winter Olympic Games. It regularly qualifies for other top-rated competitions like the World Championship. The Czech Extraliga is the key ice hockey league in the Czech Republic. Each year, many of its players transfer to the North American National Hockey League (NHL). There are fifty-seven Czech hockey players in the NHL (as of 2009), making Czechs the third largest group in the NHL, after Canadians and Americans.

Football (soccer) is another national pastime. The Czech National Football Team qualified for the 2008 UEFA European Football Championship (the Euro 2008). They have played in the Euro many times since 1960 and won the championship (as Czechoslovakia) in 1976. Although their performance hasn't been as strong in recent years, people still support this and other home sports teams as a source of national pride.

Chimney Climbing

Whether or not chimney climbing is a sport is for you to judge! The Czech Republic is probably the only country in the world where people climb factory chimneys and cooling towers as a recreational activity. There's even an official Union of Czech Chimney Climbers. These brave souls not only have fun; they also help with chimney maintenance and preservation. At the very least, they get an incredible view of whatever is around them from the top of the chimney!

Czechs at the Olympics

Czechs have competed at the Olympic Games since 1920—first as Czechoslovakia and, since 1994, as the Czech Republic. Athletes from the Czech Republic have won thirty-three medals at the Summer Olympic Games and ten medals at the Winter Olympics. Thirteen of the medals were gold, with canoeing, athletics, shooting, cross-country skiing, and ice hockey being the top sports.

Favorite Toys and Games

These days, Czech kids are just as likely as anyone in the Western world to be playing video games and downloading music onto their MP3 players. There is still a great love for wooden toys handcrafted by Czech artisans, however. These include pull toys, walking animals, hanging mobiles in the shape of birds, cars, planes, and "push-up" animals that collapse when you push the platform they're standing on and straighten back up when you let go. Handmade puzzles are also favorites.

Those who like a little challenge play chess, which is popular in many European countries. It's played competitively and for fun. Players who win in local chess festivals might even have their eye on competing in the World School Chess Team Championships.

GREECE

WELCOME TO GREECE!

More than 5,000 years old, Greece is called the Cradle of European Civilization. It was once known primarily for giving the world philosophy, democracy, and the Olympic Games. Now, this ancient land is earning an international reputation. It is becoming a global.energy hub. It has the largest fleet in the world. The 2004 Summer Olympic Games highlighted not only its beauty, but its global importance. It's no surprise that this gateway to South-Eastern Europe has become rightfully known as "Wonderful Greece." It has one foot in the 21st century and one foot in its fascinating past.

FAST FACTS

Official Name:	Hellenic Republic
Location:	Southern Europe. It borders the Aegean Sea, Ionian Sea, and the Mediterranean Sea, between Albania and Turkey.
Population:	10,749,943 (2010 estimate)
Capital City:	Athens
Area:	50,949 square miles. Greece is slightly smaller than the state of Alabama.
Major Language:	Greek
Major Religion:	Greek Orthodox: 98%
Currency:	The euro (€) (bank notes and coins) 1 euro = 100 euro-cents
Climate:	Temperate with mild, wet winters and hot, dry summers
The Land:	Mostly mountains with ranges extending into the sea in the form of peninsulas or island chains. Greece is one of the most mountainous countries in Europe.
Type of Government:	Parliamentary republic
Flag:	There are nine equal horizontal stripes of blue alternating with white. The blue square in the upper hoist side corner bears a white cross that symbolizes Greek Orthodoxy, the country's religion.
National Emblem:	A blue shield with a white cross totally surrounded by two laurel branches.
National Animal:	Dolphin
Motto:	"Freedom or Death"

Natural Environment

Greece is at the southeastern edge of Europe. It covers the southernmost part of the Balkan Peninsula. Albania, Yugoslavia, and Bulgaria form its northern border. Turkey, on the eastern shore of the Aegean Sea, stretches from northern Greece south to Crete, the country's largest island. On the west coast, the Ionian Sea separates Greece from southern Italy. Mountains that form part of the Alpine range stretch from northwest to southeast Greece.

Mount Olympus

Greece is loosely divided into northern, central, and southern areas, along with the Greek islands. The high mountains of the mainland have poor, infertile, rocky soil. The Pindus Mountains begin at the northern border and extend the length of the eastern border. The Grammos Mountains are in the northwest. The highest peak is Mount Olympus (in central Greece), at 9,570 feet. The early Greeks believed the gods lived there. While the mountains protected the country from northern invasions, they also isolated the Greeks from each other. This explains why ancient Greece was composed of many city-states (in effect, independent countries), rather than being one united state.

The long, narrow Gulf of Corinth separates the Peloponnesus Peninsula from the rest of the Greek mainland. The Corinth Canal, which was completed in 1893, was built to connect the Gulf of Corinth and the Saronic Gulf in the Aegean Sea. Delphi, an ancient sanctuary dedicated to the god Apollo and now a modern Greek town, is situated on the slopes of Mt. Parnassus high above the Gulf of Corinth.

The largest plains in Greece are Macedonia, Thessaly, and Thrace; all are near the Aegean Sea. Thessaly in particular has much fertile soil and is considered the breadbasket of Greece. Only 30 percent of the rest of the land in Greece can support crops.

The earthquakes that originally created Greece are still a problem. Greece has the most earthquakes of any country in the world. Fortunately, most of them are mild (although there were several strong quakes in 2008 and 2009). Modern buildings are constructed to be earthquake safe.

One-fifth of Greece is made up of more than 1,400 islands. Of these, only 166 are inhabited. The four main island groups are the Cyclades (sic-la-dēs), Dodecanese, Sporades (spor-a-dēs), and Ionian.

Most of the large mainland towns lie around natural harbors or in lowlands near the coast. Piraeus, on the outskirts of Athens, handles most of the commercial shipping.

Plants and Animals

Greek farmers grow olives, grapes, wheat, barley, maize, sugar beets, alfalfa, cotton, tomatoes, and other fruits and vegetables. They also raise cattle, pigs, sheep, goats, poultry, horses, mules, donkeys, and even some buffalo.

Other animals found in Greece are largely a mix of those found in Europe, Asia, and Africa. It's not unusual to see a group of graceful dolphins racing along in the water. Wolves, jackals, wild cats, foxes, wild goats, and hares are among the animals found in Greece, along with the occasional bear. There are 107 species of freshwater fish.

Much of the flora in Greece consists of white poplar, oak, chestnut, cypress, pine, fir, and olive trees. You'll also see a great many wildflowers like violets, tulips, peonies, and primroses.

Natural resources that are mined include iron, nickel, bitumen, marble, slate, and oil. Deep sea divers collect sponges, which are popular with locals and tourists alike and are often sold from vendor carts.

A History of Greece

Ancient Greece

Minoan Civilization (3000–1450 BCE)

The earliest recorded history of Greece begins around 3000 BCE. Greek civilization began on Crete, the largest island in the Aegean Sea. People on Crete built ships, made pottery and silver, and began to trade with Egypt. By 1600 BCE, they had built a lavish palace at Knossos, known through myth as the palace of King Minos.

Mycenae and the Bronze Age (1500–1150 BCE)

The Bronze Age began on the mainland of Greece, known as Hellas. By 1500 BCE, the people were building heavily fortified cities. Mycenae (mī-sē-nē) in southern Greece was the largest city. Agamemnon, its mythical king, was the most powerful ruler on the mainland. These mainland Greeks attacked and captured the palace settlements of the Minoans around 1450 BCE.

Around 1150 BCE, invaders from the north destroyed the cities and began their own occupation. Aeolians, Ionians, and Dorians swept through the south and conquered nearly the entire Peloponnesus region.

Age of Expansion (800–625 BCE)

By 750 BCE, the population of Greece had grown so large that many people left the mainland. Greek colonists settled throughout the Mediterranean, and trade increased.

The Archaic and Classical Periods (625–335 BCE)

Persia, under Cyrus the Great, was the strongest military power in the world. Darius I of Persia decided to invade Greece. A storm wrecked his fleet in 491 BCE, but he tried again two years later. The outnumbered Greek army defeated the Persians on the plains of Marathon.

The Persians did not give up easily. A second Persian army commanded by Xerxes (zerx-ēs), the son of Darius, captured Athens and burned the great Acropolis. The Greeks had their revenge one year later by defeating the Persian army at Plataea and again at Mycale. This was a turning point in history. If the Persians had defeated the Greeks, they likely would have gone on to conquer the rest of Europe. If this had happened, Western civilization as we know it may never have existed.

Beginning in 460 BCE, Athens enjoyed a Golden Age called the Classical Period. (This is the period for which ancient Greece is best known.) Sculptors, architects, and dramatists produced fine works that are still studied and honored today. Under Pericles, Athens became the artistic center of Greece.

During the Classical Period, Greece was composed of city-states that were essentially independent countries. The largest of these was Athens, followed by Sparta and Thebes. As the power of Athens grew, the city-state of Sparta became fearful of it. Sparta organized an army, led its citizens into battle, and defeated Athens in 404 BCE. But Sparta's rule was short lived. Sparta was so harsh on the other city-states of Greece that the Thebans rebelled and defeated Sparta. However, the Thebans were not strong rulers, and Greece's power began to wane.

The Hellenistic Period (335–200 BCE)

In the north, Macedonia was growing in strength. Under Phillip II, the Macedonians defeated the Spartans and reorganized Greece. Beginning in 335 BCE, Phillip's son, Alexander the Great, combined the Macedonians and Greeks into one army and attacked the Persian Empire. In ten years, Alexander conquered many surrounding lands.

Alexander is one of ancient history's most famous and colorful characters. Many admired him for his strong leadership. He certainly was an incredible leader who kept Greek civilization alive and constantly expanding. He founded new cities in Asia, India, and the Middle East and created centers of Greek culture. He promoted the sciences. Thanks to him, Greek became the language of business and helped to unite the people of a very diverse area.

Gods and Goddesses

The ancient Greeks did not always understand why the winds blew, or why it rained, or how crops grew year after year. They tried to explain events in nature by assigning each important function to a god or goddess. In case they missed honoring an important deity, the Greeks held an annual "Festival of Unknown Gods." The greatest of the Greek gods lived on Mount Olympus.

King of the Gods: Zeus
God of Sun and Youth: Apollo
God of War: Ares
God of the Sea: Poseidon
God of Love: Eros
God of Time: Kronos
God of the Underworld: Pluto
Messenger of the Gods: Hermes
Queen of the Gods: Hera
Goddess of Agriculture: Demeter
Goddess of the Moon and Hunting: Artemis
Goddess of Wisdom: Athena
Goddess of Love and Beauty: Aphrodite
Goddess of the Home: Hestia

Apollo

There are counterparts for these deities in Roman, Norse, and Egyptian mythology.

Artemis

Roman Rule (200 BCE–470 CE)

Alexander died at the age of 32 in 323 BCE. Historians are still not sure whether he was assassinated by poisoning or died from illness. After his death, his kingdom grew weak. The Romans easily conquered Greece and Macedonia around 200 BCE. Greece became a Roman province called Achaea (a-kē-a). Under Roman rule, Greece enjoyed 300 years of peace.

Alexander the Great

The Byzantine Empire (470–1453)

Christianity spread to Greece. Constantine the Great moved the capital of the Roman Empire to Byzantium and named it Constantinople. The Byzantine civilization was a continuation of the ancient Greek civilization, with Roman and Eastern influences. Its main identifying factor was the Christian religion, which shaped its entire culture. The Byzantine emperors converted the people of neighboring regions to Christianity.

The Byzantine Empire, the second great stage in Greek history, lasted about 1,000 years. It ended in 1453 CE, when the Ottoman Turks captured Constantinople.

Ottoman Rule (1453–1827)

The Turks allowed the Greeks to keep a form of self-government, mainly through their church. On March 25, 1821, the Greeks organized against the Turks and declared their independence. They fought for more than seven years to achieve independence.

In 1827, Great Britain, France, Russia, and others gave Greece military support. They combined their naval forces to defeat the Turkish fleet at the Battle of Navarino off Peloponnesus on October 20, 1827.

Greek Independence and the Modern State (1827 – present day)

In 1832, Britain, France, and Russia chose German Prince Otto I to be the first King of Greece. But in 1862, the Greeks revolted. The Greek National Assembly then chose the Prince of Denmark as ruler; He became King George I of Greece in 1863.

In 1912, Greece, Serbia, Bulgaria, and Montenegro formed an alliance against Turkey. After the Alliance defeated Turkey, Greece won Crete and other islands, as well as a large part of Macedonia.

When World War I began in 1914, Greece declared itself neutral. King Constantine favored the Germans, while Parliament and the majority of the Greek people backed England and France. In 1917, Greek liberals overthrew King Constantine and crowned his son, Alexander. The Greek prime minister then brought Greece into World War I on the side of the Allies (which included the United States) in 1917. When Alexander died, Constantine returned from exile, but again fell out of favor.

Greece was a republic from 1925 to 1935, but returned to being a monarchy under George II. In 1936, the King, motivated by political unrest, appointed Joannes Metaxas dictator for life. During World War II, Greece again declared itself neutral. In 1940, however, the Italian dictator Benito Mussolini, who was aligned with the Germans, demanded the use of Greek boats for battle. When the Greeks refused, they were invaded by Italy and Germany.

During the war, the Greek people suffered terrible hardships that left the country in turmoil. In 1946, the Greeks voted to return King George to the throne. Upon his death in 1947, his brother Paul became king.

The Greek military took control of the government in 1967. Constantine II remained head of state, but he was powerless. During this period, a military dictatorship suspended freedom of the press, parliamentary elections, and many individual rights. By 1974, however, Greece had free elections.

Greece Today

Today, Greece is a democratic republic with two main political parties. No longer isolated from the world, it is an increasingly multicultural society. You'll find migrants and retirees from Africa, Asia, England, European Union (EU) countries, and the Balkans.

Greece became part of the EU in 1983. Since then it has undergone an incredible transformation. It once was a low-tech farming society where owning a car was a privilege only for the rich. Now it's in the Information Age, with Internet cafés all over the country and car ownership a norm.

Tourists from all over the world are discovering this beautiful land. And they're not disappointed! The mountains are perfect for hiking, the beaches perfect for water sports. The ancient ruins are perfect for exploring. Greece is now one of the world's prime vacation spots!

Despite hurling themselves into the 21st century, Greeks keep their heritage very much alive. No matter how modern the country has become, visitors will always get a warm welcome along with a glimpse into an ancient past.

Daily Life

The sunshine and warm weather of Greece make it easy for both rural and urban folks to spend much of the day outside.

The Family Unit

The family unit is very important in Greece, as it has been for centuries. Although family roles are beginning to change with the demands of life in the 21st century, they remain very traditional. Men are still the main income earners. Women may work outside the home, but their household and childcare duties come first. They will probably also take care of elderly family members.

Urban and Rural Life

About one-third of the people in Greece live in the capital of Athens, one of the world's oldest cities. In cities such as Athens, many people live in apartment buildings. Many family members may live in the same building. Although the population of the villages is declining, life for those who remain in them is much the same as it was many years ago. While motor scooters are a popular form of transportation on narrow city streets, people in the villages may still ride donkeys—especially on the small islands or on steep mountain roads.

The outer walls of many apartments and homes are whitewashed twice a year to prevent sun damage. Wooden window and door frames are painted a bright color—usually blue. Passages between homes and buildings are very narrow. Where there is no room for gardening, pots of flowers and herbs fill the window sills and steps.

Most families in the city own at least one car. Since there are not many parking facilities available for the houses and apartment buildings in the city, people usually park on the street. Due to traffic, it's not as common as it once was for mothers to chat to neighbors while the kids play nearby. Children play in designated areas that serve as playgrounds and gathering places for adults.

Going to School

The Greek government provides free and mandatory education for children between the ages of four and 15. Any child above the age of four must go to kindergarten. (Many kids go to preschool as well, but this isn't required.) Kids start primary school at age six and stay there until age 12. From ages 12 to 15, they attend the gymnasium, studying history, literature, and geography in addition to basic subjects like science and math. Kids attend school from 8:00 AM to 2:00 PM, five days a week. Summer vacation is from the end of June to mid-September.

There are two types of post-secondary schools: unified upper secondary schools that focus on academic subjects or technical-vocational schools that focus on job skills. Students finish secondary school at age 18.

There are two major universities in Athens and one at Thessaloniki (also called Salonica), the second largest city in Greece. The University of Athens offers schools of art, archaeology, business, and others. Being admitted to a public Greek university is determined by performance on exams administered by the government. Some private universities have campuses in Greece. But these are mostly foreign schools whose degrees are not recognized by the Greek state.

Famous Greeks

There are so many famous people of Greek descent that it would take pages to give even a brief bit of information about each one. Here are a few names you might recognize.

Britain's Prince Philip, Duke of Edinburgh (1921–) and husband of Queen Elizabeth II since 1947, was originally a royal prince of Greece and Denmark.

George Stephanopoulos (stef-a-nop-o-lus) (1961–) is an American broadcaster who first came to public attention as a political advisor in President Bill Clinton's administration. As of 2009, he remains the ABC News Chief Washington Correspondent and appears on his own weekly TV show.

Aristotle Onassis (1906–1975) was a famous shipping magnate of the 20th century and one of the richest men in the world. He is best known, however, for marrying former first lady Jacqueline Kennedy several years after the assassination of President John F. Kennedy.

Spiro T. Agnew (1918–1996) was the 39th Vice President of the United States, serving under President Richard Nixon. He was the first Greek-American Vice President. He was also the 55th Governor of the state of Maryland.

Maria Callas (1923–1977) was an American-born Greek and one of the most famed opera singers of the 20th century.

Christopher Sarantakos (1967–), better known as Criss Angel, is of Greek descent. A magician, he is well known for his awesome feats of illusion on his TV show, *Criss Angel Mindfreak*.

Nia Vardalos (1962—) is a Greek-Canadian actress and writer who explored traditional Greek family roles in the famous film *My Big Fat Greek Wedding*.

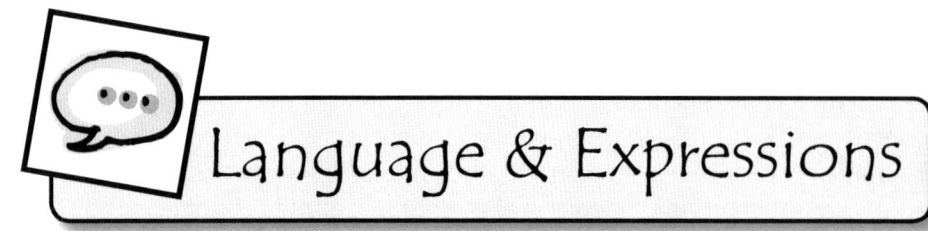

Language & Expressions

Here are some fun facts about verbal and nonverbal communication in Greece.

Famous Greek Proverbs

Here are ten famous Greek proverbs. What do you think they mean?

If you do not have brains, you follow the same route twice.
All things good to know are difficult to learn.
The beginning is the half of every action.
From a thorn comes a rose, and from a rose comes a thorn.
The heart that loves is always young.
There is no need to teach an eagle to fly.
Observe your enemies, for they first find your faults.
An iron rod bends while it is hot.
Act quickly, think slowly.
Add not fire to fire.

Body Language and Etiquette in Greece

Here are some examples of body language and etiquette you'll find in Greece.

Use a firm handshake when first meeting both men and women. If you are being introduced to a family, shake hands with the children, too.

If you are good friends with a woman, you may greet her with a hug and a kiss on each cheek. If you are good friends with a man, you may greet him with a pat on the shoulder or on the back.

Greek people gesture a lot in conversation.

Making the "okay" sign with your thumb and forefinger is a rude gesture in Greece. It's acceptable, however, to give the "thumbs up" sign.

People signal "yes" with a slight nod of the head downward. They signal "no" with a slight bob of the head upward.

When invited to a Greek home, arrive about 30 minutes after the stated time of the dinner or get-together. Be sure to take a small gift for your host, like flowers, candy, or some pastries.

Your host or fellow guests might share the food from their plates with you! It is considered good manners to offer to share some of your own food.

Take your shoes off before entering someone's home.

Know before You Go

Sometime around 800 BCE, the Greeks adapted the alphabet of the Phoenicians, an ancient trading culture that spread across the Mediterranean from 1550 to 300 BCE. There were no symbols for vowels in the Phoenician alphabet, so the Greeks added them. The Greek alphabet of 24 letters became the basis for alphabets of the Romans and all other Europeans. Below is the Greek alphabet along with the name of each letter.

Α	α	alpha		Ν	ν	nu
Β	β	beta		Ξ	ξ	xi
Γ	γ	gamma		Ο	ο	omicron
Δ	δ	delta		Π	π	pi
Ε	ε	epsilon		Ρ	ρ	rho
Ζ	ζ	zeta		Σ	σ, ς	sigma
Η	η	eta		Τ	τ	tau
Θ	θ	theta		Υ	υ	upsilon
Ι	ι	iota		Φ	φ	phi
Κ	κ	kappa		Χ	χ	chi
Λ	λ	lambda		Ψ	ψ	psi
Μ	μ	mu		Ω	ω	omega

Here are some common phrases you will use in Greece. The Greek spelling, transcription, and pronunciation are also given. Try them out! Look up some additional ones!

English	**Greek**	**Transcription**	**Pronunciation**
yes	ναί	nai	nay
no	οχί	ochi	ohi
goodbye	αντίο	antio	addio
good luck	καλή τύχη	kali tuxi	kali tihi
How are you?	Τι κάνεις;	ti kaneis	ti kanis
please	παρακαλώ	parakalo	parakalo
thank you	ευχαριστώ	euxaristo	efharisto
What is your name?	Πώς σε λένε;	pos se lene	pos se lene
What time is it?	Τι ώρα είνε;	ti ora eine	ti ora ine

Days of the week:

Monday	Δευτέρα	Deutera	deftera
Tuesday	Τρίτη	Triti	triti
Wednesday	Τετάρτη	Tetarti	tetarti
Thursday	Πέμπτη	Pempti	pempti
Friday	Παρασκευή	Paraskevi	paraskevi
Saturday	Σαββατο	Sabbato	savato
Sunday	Κυριακή	Kuriaki	kiriaki

Numbers:

one	ένα	ena	ena
two	δύο	duo	dhio
three	τρία	tria	tria
four	τέσσερα	tessara	tessara
five	πέντε	pente	pendhe
six	έξι	exi	exi
seven	εφτά	ephta	ephta
eight	οκτώ	okto	okto
nine	εννέα	ennea	ennea
ten	δέκα	deka	dheka

MP5126 – Greece

Name _____ Date _____

GREEK ROOTS, PREFIXES, AND SUFFIXES

Many words in English have Greek roots, prefixes, or suffixes. Write one English word for each root, prefix, or suffix listed below.

ROOT WORDS

Root Word	Meaning	Example
1. agri	field	_____
2. athl	prize	_____
3. dem	people	_____
4. path	feeling, suffering	_____
5. ped	child	_____

PREFIXES

Prefix	Meaning	Example
6. auto	self-same	_____
7. geo	earth	_____
8. hyper	excessive	_____
9. micro	small	_____
10. thermo	heat	_____

SUFFIXES

Suffix	Meaning	Example
11. graphy	writing or field of study	_____
12. metry	measuring device	_____
13. oid	resembling, like, or shaped	_____
14. ology	science, theory, or study	_____
15. phone	sound	_____

FOODS

A History of Great Food!

Greece has a long history of appreciating good food and the people who create it. In ancient Greece, cooks were highly respected and rewarded with money and land for creating new dishes. A love of food is still a cornerstone of Greek culture. Whether eating in a friendly restaurant, tavern, or dining at home on the patio, Greeks love to eat!

Daily Meals

Greeks eat a light breakfast of fruit, cheese, bread, and strong coffee. They eat a light lunch around 1:00 PM in the cities; in the country, this is often the main meal. Between 1:00 and 2:00 PM, school kids rest and some businesses close for afternoon rest. Later in the afternoon, coffee and cheese tarts are served at outdoor cafes. The entire family gathers as late as 10:00 PM for a simple evening meal that might include bread, dried figs, and fish. Shrimp, squid, lobster, and octopus are some of the local catches made into savory dishes.

Common Foods

Meats and Fish

The most common meats in Greece are lamb, pork, beef, goat, and chicken. Many Greek dishes contain meat that has been ground up and baked or stewed with vegetables such as tomatoes and spices such as garlic. The final dish is often topped with a savory sauce.

There are some exceptions to this, however. Whole roasted lamb or whole roasted suckling pig, both of which are traditional at Easter and Christmas, are sometimes served. Grilled pork chops and steaks are also popular.

Greece is a seafood-lover's paradise! There's a type of seafood for every taste, including sardines, calamari (squid), octopus, mussels, swordfish, and lobster. Some of the seafood is imported from the United States, China, and elsewhere. Nonetheless, it's fixed Greek-style. Grilled, fried, or fixed in appetizers, casseroles, soups, and stews are just some of the ways you'll get seafood in Greece. In smaller restaurants you may even follow your waiter to the kitchen to see which fish is available. Go to the Athens Central Market any weekday morning to see the vast assortment of fish available from Greece and the Mediterranean.

Breads

Greeks love bread and bake many different kinds, from plain to elaborately braided and shaped loaves. In small towns, some families are without ovens, so they mix and shape the dough at home and take it to the local baker to finish.

Bread is eaten at every meal in a variety of ways. It can be dipped in olive oil or one of a variety of sauces, such as *tsatziki* (garlic-cucumber-yogurt dip) or *melitzana salata* (eggplant sauce). Many village bakeries still use wood-burning stoves and bake with the recipes handed down through generations. They produce the familiar pita bread used for sandwiches and dips. *Paximadia* (the Greek word for *biscuit*) is hardy breakfast bread that is just right for dipping in hot milk or coffee. There are also different breads for different holidays and festivals, like the Easter bread that has a red Easter egg baked into the middle of it.

Olives and Olive Oil

Greek olives are some of the best in the world. They have been a staple of the Greek diet for thousands of years. The ancient Greeks ate black olives and believed them to be a healthy food. As it turns out, they were right! Olives are high in iron, Vitamin E, and fiber. They're one of the healthiest foods on the planet!

People in Greece have their favorite olives—and there are many varieties to choose from. But the olive we usually associate with Greece is the black Kalamata that comes with the Greek salads you get in the United States.

Like Greek olives, Greek olive oil is outstanding. Greeks consume more olive oil per person than people in any other country in the world. It's not hard to see why. Olive oil is a staple in Greek cooking and is used in everything from appetizers to main dishes and desserts. People dip bread in it, pour it over fish, flavor soups and stews with it, and put it in salads. The olives are hand-picked in late November and taken to a pressing plant where the oil is extracted. Today, Greek olive oil is exported to countries all over the world. It's a significant contributor to the Greek economy.

Fruits and Vegetables

There may not be much farmland in Greece, but the land that *is* used produces some of the tastiest fruits and vegetables in the world.

The tomato is one of the most important fruits in Greek cuisine. It's eaten raw, sliced and covered with olive oil. It's also cooked into a number of dishes, made into sauces, or stuffed with a savory mixture of rice and meat.

Like tomatoes, peppers are found on just about everyone's table. Peppers are served raw, sliced into salads, grilled, fried, or stirred into baked or stewed dishes. Stuffed peppers are often served with stuffed tomatoes.

Potatoes are a staple of the Greek diet and thicken lots of different stews. Oven-roasted potatoes are often prepared with large pieces of meat like roast lamb or chicken and flavored with onions, garlic, and olive oil. Potatoes fried in olive oil are topped with lemon and salt. *Potato salat* is a lighter version of potato salad, seasoned with oil, lemon, and onions.

Many types of beans are nutritious and delicious additions to soups, salads, and stews, including lentils, large white broad beans, and fava beans. Greece is famous for its *fassoulada,* a white bean soup called the "national food of the Greeks."

Onions, garlic, eggplant, zucchini, beets, and spinach are just some of the other vegetables that figure heavily into Greek cuisine.

Many Greek meals end with a plate of sliced fruit like watermelon, honeydew melon, apples, pears, cherries, and oranges. Giant juicy figs, which ripen in August and September, are always a welcome treat, whether bought at the market or plucked from a local tree. Grapes grow well in Greek's climate and have been a part of the Greek economy for centuries.

Cheese

Greece has hundreds of goats, sheep, and cows—and an incredible variety of cheeses made from their milk. No matter where you go in Greece, every area has its own local cheese and cheese-makers.

Probably the most familiar Greek cheese is crumbly feta (white goat cheese), the unofficial national cheese of Greece. It's so popular that some cheese shops in Greece sell only feta. It is used in many Greek dishes, including Greek Salad and *spanakopita* (spinach pie). It has a distinctive, rich taste.

Kasseri is another rich cheese made of sheep or goat milk. It's served as an appetizer, sliced and eaten plain. It's also baked or deep-fried. Any way you eat it, it's delicious! Other varieties of hard cheese are grated into pasta dishes or salads.

Herbs and Spices

Most of the herbs and spices used in Greek recipes originated in the Mediterranean or Western Asia. Originally cloves, cinnamon, cassia, pepper, mace, and nutmeg were used only in medicines, body salves, and perfumes. Later, Greeks began to experiment with spices to add more flavor to food. Listed below are some spices and their uses.

Basil – Greeks plant a few seeds of basil, known as the herb of royalty, outside their kitchen doors to grow for flavoring soups, stews, and salads. Basil is also grown to give to visitors as protection against harm.
Bay Leaf (Laurel) – Leaves are added to meat, fish, or stew. In early Greece, laurel wreaths were placed on the heads of winning athletes.
Cassia – Similar to cinnamon. In ancient times both cassia and cinnamon were so valuable that they were included with ivory, gold, and camels as gifts for conquerors.
Clove – Cloves were prized for their oil, which was used to make medicine. Today, cloves are used to season a variety of Greek dishes.
Mint – Mint is used in cooking and is grown extensively.
Lemon – Brought to Greece from Palestine, lemon is the most important fruit flavoring in Greek cooking.
Thyme – Once considered food for the poor and slaves, thyme was used by the rich in cosmetics. Today it is used to flavor lamb, fish, and some fowl.
Sage – A tea is made from the leaves of one variety of sage that grows in the mountains.

Menu

These traditional and tasty dishes are sure to be on the menu of most Greek restaurants you visit. Try one—or several!

Soups, Salads, Appetizers
Avgolemono: A soup made with eggs, lemon juice, and chicken
Fakes: Lentil soup served with vinegar and feta cheese
Fasolada: Bean soup with tomatoes, carrots, celery, and olive oil
Greek Salad: A bowl of lettuce packed with chunks of feta cheese, tomatoes, olives, onions, and green peppers tossed in an olive oil dressing
Psarosoupa: Fish soup
Saganak: Fried cheese
Taramosalata: A delicious creamy spread for pita bread made with fish roe, bread crumbs, and olive oil

Greek Salad

Main Dishes
Aginares (ahg- ee-nar-as) a la Polita: Artichokes with olive oil
Dolmades: Grape leaves stuffed with ground lamb, rice, and herbs
Gyros (Eur-ōs): A pita bread sandwich filled with meat roasted on a vertical spit and served with tzatziki sauce (garlic-cucumber-yogurt dip), tomatoes, and onions
Moussaka: A casserole of ground lamb, eggplant, and rich white sauce
Pastitsio: A layered casserole of macaroni and chopped meat topped with a rich custard sauce
Spanakopita: Spinach pie—a savory spinach filling in a triangle of flaky pastry
Souvlaki: Marinated meat such as lamb, chicken, pork, or fish (such as swordfish or shrimp) grilled on a skewer

Spanakopita

Desserts
Baklava: Pastry layers of nuts, sugar, honey or syrup, and cloves
Karidopita: A walnut cake
Koulourakia (koo-loo-ra-kia): Butter or olive oil cookies
Yogurt: Usually served with honey or fruit syrup

Baklava

RECIPE - FRUIT AND YOGURT

Ingredients
- 4 cups chopped fresh fruit (grapes, orange slices, peaches, berries, and melon)
- 1 cup slivered almonds
- 1 cup plain low fat yogurt
- 2 tablespoons honey
- Optional: 1½ tablespoons grated lemon rind

Directions
1. Combine the yogurt, honey, and lemon rind in a medium bowl.
2. Put the fruit and almonds in a serving bowl. Stir the mixture gently.
3. Pour the yogurt mixture over fruit.
4. Serve each portion in a small bowl or paper cup.

Holidays & Festivals

People all over Greece celebrate the national holidays. Many communities have local festivals that celebrate Greek history, patron saints, the arts, the local harvest, or music and dance. Delicious food, traditional customs, historical reenactments, singing, dance, wearing folk costumes, and offering best wishes for good fortune highlight these celebrations.

New Year's Day, the Feast of St. Basil • *January 1*

St. Basil is the Greek version of Santa Claus. Some families leave a log in the fireplace for him to step on as he slips down the chimney.

Everyone in Greece celebrates this happy day, looking for a great start to the New Year. Gifts are exchanged. According to an old Byzantine custom, people share a New Year's cake with a coin baked into it. The person who finds the lucky coin in his or her slice will have good luck in the coming year.

There may also be a renewal of waters ritual in which all water jugs in the house are refilled with new St. Basil's Water. Some people also conduct a ceremony with offerings to the spirits of springs and fountains.

The Epiphany • *January 6*

On this day, the Eastern Orthodox Church celebrates the baptism of Jesus Christ. This is marked throughout Greece by a Blessing of the Waters. A cross is thrown into the local waters and retrieved by swimmers brave enough to dive into the chilly waves. The swimmers are said to receive good luck for their efforts. This event is particularly spectacular in Piraeus, the major seaport of Greece, and in other waterfront towns.

Apokrias • *Mid-February*

Apokrias, the Carnival Season, lasts two weeks. It is similar to Mardi Gras and Halloween. The festival is all about dressing up, having fun, eating, partying, and generally having a great time before the somber time of Lent. People throw parties and wear masks, wigs, and funny or scary costumes. They often carry streamers, throw confetti, and make lots of noise. The party atmosphere goes on day and night. Kids run in costume to the houses of neighbors, who try to guess their identities. The kids get sweets, but they also do tricks like throwing confetti and streamers on the neighbors' houses. Apokrias ends with Grand Carnival Parades all over Greece.

Greek National Anniversary (Greek Independence Day) • *March 25*

This major holiday celebrates Greece's victory in the war of independence against the Turks in 1821. Larger towns and cities hold military parades.

The Easter Season • *April or May*

Easter is the major Greek Orthodox celebration of the year. It is more important than Christmas.

On Holy Thursday, people traditionally prepare sweet buns and color eggs red with onion skin or special red dyes. The egg symbolizes the renewal of life, and the red color symbolizes the blood of Christ.

Good Friday is a day to reflect on the death of Christ. The churches are draped in black. People do not do household chores or cook meals. In each city, town, or village, there is a funeral procession in which four men carry a bier through the streets to symbolize the burial of Christ. People in the procession carry candles.

On Holy Saturday evening, bells ring out all over Greece as ceremonies of the resurrection take place in front of the churches. People light candles and then go home after the Easter midnight church service for the traditional feast of Easter lamb soup.

Easter Sunday is a joyous celebration with the traditional meal of lamb roasted on a spit. People eat the red Easter eggs. They first crack the eggs against each other. The person with the last uncracked egg will have good luck. People celebrate late into the night.

On the island of Crete, there is a special Easter Sunday celebration in which an effigy of Judas Iscariot, who betrayed Christ, is burned in a bonfire. During Holy Week, people will gather wood in preparation for the bonfire.

International Workers Day • *May 1*

International Workers Day is similar to Labor Day. It celebrates workers' achievements. People usually gather for a rally (or a protest!).

May 1st is also the beginning of the many flower festivals held throughout Greece. Balconies, stairs, and street corners are decorated with masses of spring flowers. Even the local donkeys wear hats, flowers, and strings of colorful beads around their necks. The island of Rhodes is particularly well known for its flower festival that it hosts in its capital at the end of May.

Feast of the Assumption • *August 15*

This day honors the Virgin Mary's entrance into heaven. Next to Easter, the Feast of the Assumption is the biggest religious holiday in Greece. On the island of Tinos, thousands of people from all over Greece crawl on their knees up the steps to the church that holds the holy icon of Mary. There are religious ceremonies held at most other churches in Greece, as well as parties afterward.

Ohi Day • *October 28*

Also called "No" Day, this holiday celebrates the anniversary of the Greek defeat of the invading Italian army in 1940, during World War II. Major towns and cities hold military parades.

The Christmas Season

Christmas trees are becoming more common, although they are usually artificial as opposed to fresh-cut live trees. People put them up in mid-December, and decorate them with tinsel and a star on top. They decorate their homes and balconies with colorful lights; most cities and towns have colorful Christmas displays. Even boats are decorated!

On December 23rd, the citizens of Kozani (in northern Greece) honor the shepherds who lit the bonfires to announce the birth of Christ. This ceremony takes place in the village of Siatista, where people light bonfires and dance around them. Prizes are awarded to those who created the three best bonfires.

On December 24, Christmas Eve, young children go door-to-door singing carols for sweets or dried fruits. Families gather together to eat a traditional meal of roast pig and sweet Christ Bread. The crusts of the large loaves are engraved and frosted with symbols that reflect the family's profession.

Christmas morning begins with an early church service. After the service, Greeks feast on stuffed roast turkey or roast suckling pig. Traditional sweets like *baklava* round out the meal.

New Years Eve is spent much like celebrations all over the world. There are parties with dancing, singing, live music, and lots of food! Many cities have fireworks.

Creative Arts

Folk Music, Folk Dance, and Folk Costumes

Music and dance are at the very heart of Greek life. Any time is a good time to sing, play an instrument, or dance. Even Sunday dinner at a local taverna may end with a dance around the restaurant—and everyone is expected to join in!

Greek folk music is said to have come from ancient Greece, where boys were taught music from the age of six. Today, folk music is played and sung all over Greece, with each region contributing its own special character to the songs. Certain instruments give Greek folk music its distinctive sound. The *bouzouki* (boo-zoo-kē) is a folk instrument similar to the guitar and popular at informal gatherings. The *santouri* is another popular instrument, called the dulcimer of the Orient.

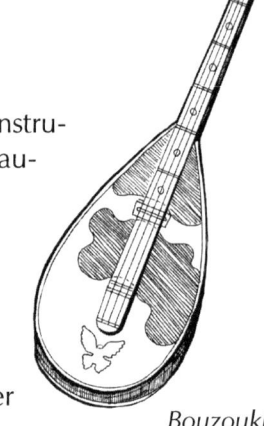
Bouzouki

An Evzone guard

Greek dance is also said to have come from the ancients. Today, there are about 4,000 traditional dances in all regions of Greece combined. Each island and mainland area has its own style and interpretation. Greek culture may be changing in the 21st century, but the primary function of Greek dance remains the same. It brings people together for holidays, harvests, social functions, festivals, weddings, and any other celebration you can imagine! Some dances are slow and deliberate, while others are fast and upbeat. In many of the dances, people hold hands and move together in a line. According to tradition, dancers are arranged by age, with the oldest at the front of the line. If you're visiting Greece and you want to join in the fun, go to the end of the line, no matter how old you are!

Each region in Greece proudly wears its own folk costume for special occasions. There are many different costumes for men, women, and children. They all feature bold color and dramatic design. One of the best places to see a common traditional Greek folk costume is at the Parliament building in Athens. The Evzone Presidential Guards, dressed in their traditional uniform of white skirts, pleated blouses, and pom-pom decorated boots, perform an hourly changing of the guard.

Famous Architecture

Most ancient cities in Greece had an *acropolis*, or high city, where the citizens honored their gods and took shelter in time of war. Many such elaborate temples were built on the hills. Roofs were supported by enormous columns. The tops of the columns were created in one of three designs (also called orders): Doric, Ionic, or Corinthian. The Doric was the simplest design; it was generally used on the mainland. The Ionic is famous for its scrolls and was found most often on the Aegean islands. The name Corinthian is derived from the Greek city of Corinth, although this design was first used in Athens. It's seldom seen in Greek architecture, however, and was far more common in Rome. It is quite fancy compared to the other two styles. All three of these styles are still used all over the world.

The best-known acropolis is the Acropolis of Athens, which is known simply as *the* Acropolis. Greeks call it the sacred rock. In 2007, the Acropolis was the leading monument on the European Cultural Heritage list of world monuments.

The Parthenon

The Parthenon was a temple in Athens that honored the goddess Athena, the city's protector. The temple of Zeus at Olympia and the Temple of Apollo at Delphi were two other famous temples of ancient Greece. The original Olympic Stadium in Athens was restored and rebuilt for the 1896 Olympic Games.

Art

Art of Ancient Greece

Many major museums throughout the world exhibit fine examples of the art of Ancient Greece, such as vases and urns used for religious purposes or as serving pieces. With their geometric designs and human and animal figures, these incredible pieces are very distinctive. Many are also extremely well preserved. You can't miss them in a display case!

Sculpture of Ancient Greece

Among the ancient Wonders of the World was the Colossus of Rhodes, a male figure that stood more than 100 feet tall at the entrance to the city's harbor. Phidias (fid-ē-us), one of the greatest sculptors of Ancient Greece, carved a statue of the god Zeus (King of the Gods) for the Temple of Zeus at Olympia. This work was also named an ancient Wonder of the World.

Phidias was also in charge of creating the sculptures for the lavishly decorated Parthenon in Athens. Many of his carved marble figures of gods and goddesses decorated the Parthenon.

Greek's Famous Master Painter

Domenikos Theotokopoulos, better known as El Greco, was born in Crete in the 16th century. He is one of the world's most famous painters. His masterpieces hang in the most prestigious museums. Although Greek by birth, he did most of his painting in Spain and got his nickname of El Greco (which means "the Greek" in Spanish) there. His painting style is so unique that most art scholars cannot categorize him according to a "school" of painting. His most famous painting is *View of Toledo*.

Folk Art

In the mountains of Greece, skilled weavers use goat wool to create rugs, blankets, and clothing. Women in both urban and rural areas embroider colorful, intricate designs on clothing, folk costumes, and other items. Silversmiths and goldsmiths make updated versions of ancient jewelry pieces, such as earrings and brooches. Beautiful gems are often added.

Drama

Ancient Greek drama, centered in Athens, flourished between 550 and 220 BC. Tragedies, comedies, and the satyr play (funny plays based in Greek mythology) were three types of plays.

A Greek Amphitheatre

Greek drama was performed outdoors. Early theaters, called amphitheaters, were built into a hillside. Many modern theaters are still built on this model. Various props were used to help tell the story. An actor might have been suspended to give the impression of flying. A wagon brought supposedly "dead" characters onstage. And pictures were dropped into a scene to give the suggestion of where the action was taking place. A chorus of many actors helped tell the story of each play. The actors spoke or sang in unison, giving information to help the audience follow the story.

Sometimes the characters wore large masks. These allowed the audience to better see the actors and helped the actors to better show a character's personality. They also allowed one actor to play more than one part by wearing a different mask. Since women were not allowed to act, the masks also allowed men to play women's parts. Some historians think that women were not even allowed to *watch* the plays! The actors also wore padded costumes, masks, and boots with heavy wooden blocks for soles. The height of the boots varied with the importance of the character.

Not all of the works written by early Greek dramatists such as Aeschylus, Sophocles, and Euripides have survived. Of those that do, many such as *Electra* and *Oedipus* (ed-i-pus) *the King* are performed throughout the world. The National Theatre of Greece in Athens performs Greek tragedies each year.

Literature

Greek literature is considered the country's greatest contribution to modern thought. One of Greece's earliest authors was Hesiod, who combined traditional myth and stories of his own to write the *Theogony*, a history of the gods. The stories in this work form the basis of Greek mythology as we know it today.

Homer, who wrote the *Iliad* and the *Odyssey*, is considered the finest Greek poet of all time. Other important Greek authors and there genres were:

Plato	philosophy
Aristophanes (air-is-tof-a-nēs)	comedy
Aristotle	philosophy
Plutarch (plu-tark)	biography
Aesop	fables

After the Greek War of Independence in the 1820s, Greeks began to lay the foundations of patriotic literature. Famous writers of this period include:

Dionysius Solomos	patriotic poetry
Emmanual Rhoides	books, journalism; wrote *Papess Joanne (Pope Joan)* in which he attempted to prove that a female Pope existed; was the first to translate Edgar Allan Poe into Greek
Kostas Palamas	combined ancient and modern folklore

Greek novelists and award-winning poets of the modern era include:

Nikos Kazantzakis	novels, including the famous *Zorba the Greek*
Yannis Ritsos	poetry
George Seferis	poetry; first Greek to win the Nobel Prize in Literature (1963)
Odysseus Elytis	poetry; won the Nobel Prize in Literature (1979)

MAKE YOUR OWN GREEK POTTERY PLATE

There are several types of ancient Greek pottery. But the one we instantly recognize is red-figure pottery in which red images or designs appear on a dark background. Make your own red-figure Greek pottery plate.

Materials
- paper plate
- tempera paints (black and red or orange)
- paintbrush
- brushes
- water bowl, water, and cloth for cleaning paint brushes

Directions
1. Paint your paper plate black. Let it dry for a few hours.

2. Paint one of the designs below onto the black plate. Or, create a design of your own. Research ancient Greek pottery designs using the Internet or other resources. You could also read a Greek myth and develop your own design.

Sports & Games

Sports

The Olympics: Games for the Ages

The Ancient Greeks believed that sports were valuable training for warfare and in honoring their gods. Given the importance of sport in the life of Ancient Greece, it's no surprise that the Olympic Games developed and endure to this day.

The first organized Olympic Games were in 776 BC. They were held in Olympia every four years after that, at the time of the full moon in August and September. In honor of Zeus, athletes came from all over Greece to participate in competitions running, jumping, throwing a javelin and a discus, wrestling, boxing, and chariot racing. Wealthy Greeks bred horses for two- and four-horse teams used in chariot races. The charioteers were professional drivers, much like jockeys are professional horse riders today.

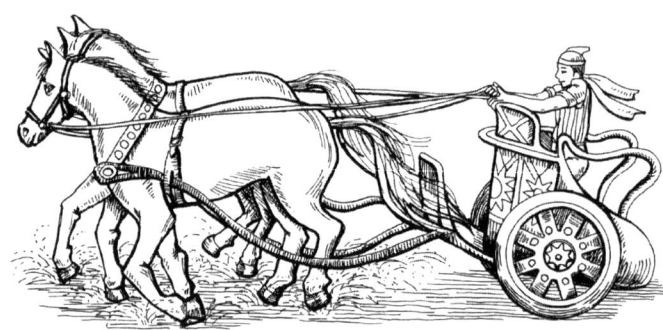

One of the foot races was based on an event in 490 BC at Marathon, near Athens. Persian warriors tried to invade Greece but were defeated at Marathon. One of the victorious Greeks ran 26 miles from Marathon to Athens to bring the good news. This was the first of the "marathons"—long-distance foot races of 26 miles. We still use the term *marathon* today. Many marathons are 26-mile races.

To qualify for the Olympics, a person had to be male, Greek, and free. (By the last Olympics in 393 AD, athletes from many other lands had become contestants.) Women and slaves were excluded from the Games. Athletes trained in a facility called a gymnasium. If an athlete won three Olympic events, he was much honored at his gymnasium.

The Olympic Games were so important that all wars stopped during the Olympics so contestants could travel back and forth to the Games. Cities that did not honor the truce were heavily fined.

The athletes were not the only ones active at the Olympics. Poets wrote odes about the champions. Philosophers read their works to the audience. Sculptors designed statues of the winners.

In 1896 the first modern Olympic Games were held in the Panathenaic Stadium near Athens. In 1996, the ceremonial torch was lit at the Temple of Zeus by a woman in a flowing Grecian gown. She handed the torch to the first runner while white doves that symbolized peace were released into the sky. The torch was passed to more than 10,000 runners until it reached Atlanta, Georgia, where it ignited the flame for the 1996 Olympic Games! More recently, Greece hosted the 2004 Olympic Games.

Football and Basketball in Greece Today

The most popular sport in modern Greece is football (soccer). Greeks are enthusiastic fans and follow their favorite teams on radio and TV. As of 2009, the Greek national football team is ranked 12th in the world. It won the 2004 UEFA European Football Championship.

Basketball closely follows soccer as a national favorite. As of 2008, the Greek national basketball team is ranked fourth in the world. It won the European Championship in 1987 and 2005 and took second place in the International Basketball Federation (FIBA) World Championships in 2006.

Other Sports

The beautiful blue waters of Greece draw many locals and tourists to water sports. Fishing, water-skiing, sailing, and wind surfing are extremely popular. Several areas sponsor rowing regattas and yacht racing.

Greek waters are filled with precious treasure from thousands of shipwrecks in Classical, Hellenic, Roman, Byzantine, and early modern times. Even entire cities are thought to exist in the waters. Although diving was once restricted, the Greek government opened up the coastline to increase tourism. Unfortunately, treasure hunters are taking valuable finds, such as coins, weapons, gold, and jewelry. The Greek government is trying to prevent this theft.

Greece is known for its heat and sunshine, but snow skiing is very popular. In season, there is downhill and cross-country skiing on Mount Olympus, Mount Parnassus, and on the Pindus Mountain slopes.

There is an extensive network of trails for mountain climbers and hikers. Spacious mountain areas are available for overnight campers.

Finally, exploring caves and bicycling along the shore or in the hills are enjoyable weekend activities. Many Greeks relax by sitting in the sun at a café table, enjoying a meal, and playing card games.

POLAND

WELCOME TO POLAND!

Poland can trace its roots back 1,000 years. Throughout the centuries, it has enjoyed independence, yet it has also been dominated by other counties. No longer under Communist rule, Poland is now taking its hard-earned place on the world stage. Foreign firms are investing in the country. Poles are finally experiencing political freedom. Despite the upheaval the Polish people have endured—particularly since World War I—their deep love of country has gotten them through very bad times. Today, that patriotic spirit is alive and thriving in Poland.

FAST FACTS

Official Name:	Republic of Poland
Location:	Central Europe, east of Germany
Population:	38,463,689 (2010 estimate)
Capital City:	Warsaw
Area:	120,726 square miles. Poland is about the size of the British Isles or the state of New Mexico.
Major Language:	Polish
Major Religions:	Roman Catholic: 89.8% (about 75% practice the religion) Eastern Orthodox: 1.3%
Currency:	Złoty (zwa-tā) 1 złoty = 100 groszy (grosh-y)
Climate:	Temperate with cloudy, fairly mild winters with frequent precipitation; mild summers with frequent rain. Temperatures average 30°F in January; summer averages 70°F in July.
The Land:	Poland is mostly a flat plain with mountains along the southern border.
Type of Government:	Republic
Flag:	Two equal horizontal bands of white (top) and red, which the Polish Constitution defines as the country's national colors.
Coat of Arms:	Poland's Coat of Arms is a white eagle with a golden beak and talons; it also wears a golden crown. The image is set on a red shield.
National Flower:	Corn Poppy (also known as the Red Poppy and Flanders Poppy)
Mottos: **(Unofficial)**	"God, Honor, Fatherland" "For our freedom and yours"

MP5126 – Poland

Natural Environment

Poland is often called the "Heart of Europe." It is the gateway to east-central Europe, with the Baltic Sea to the north, Germany to the west, the Czech and Slovak Republics to the south, Russia and Lithuania to the northeast, and Belarus and Ukraine to the east. Only in the extreme eastern part of Poland is the country similar to its eastern neighbors in structure, climate, and vegetation. Otherwise, Poland is classified as part of Western Europe.

In the south, the Sudeten Mountains and the Polish Carpathian Mountains (with their central group, the High Tatras), dominate the landscape. Mt. Rysy is the highest peak at 8,199 feet. At the foot of the beautiful Carpathians lies the Zakopane (zak-ō-pon-a), one of the best skiing and recreational areas in Poland.

Rivers are a significant geographical feature of Poland. On the western border are the Oder and Neisse Rivers. The Vistula River runs through the country and flows through the capital of Warsaw. Rivers and canals provide valuable transportation networks through Poland.

To the north is the 310-mile coastline of the Baltic Sea. This gives Poland its temperate climate and has determined its trade and relationships with its neighbors and with the rest of Europe. The Baltic has provided fish as well as beautiful amber, one of Poland's major natural resources, which the ancients used as money. Today, Poland's skilled jewelry designers incorporate amber into many of their stunning pieces.

Plants and Animals

In the northeast is Białowieza (bya-wōv-ā-za), the remainder of Europe's primeval forest that remains relatively untouched by humans. These ancient woods are home to the *wisent* (vī-zent), the Polish bison that is the biggest animal in Poland and a cousin of the American buffalo. The forests are also filled with brown bears, wild boar, eagles, falcons, deer, lynx, moose, wolves, owls, elk, and beavers.

Of the total number of birds that migrate to Europe each summer, one-fourth of them breed in Poland. You'll mostly find them in the lake districts and the wetlands along the Biebrza (byeb-za) and Narew Rivers in northeast Poland, and around the Warta River in west-central Poland. Some villages in the northeastern Masuria Lake District, which contains more than 2,000 lakes, have more storks than people!

In the west-central region of West Wielkopolska (veel-kop-ol-ska) is a unique underground bat preserve. There are dozens of miles of concrete tunnels built by the Germans between 1925 and 1941 to provide winter shelter for a few thousand bats. Bats are protected by the Polish government (and by the governments of most other European countries).

In the Polish countryside, pigs, horses, geese, ducks, and chickens are common. Sunflowers are popular, and Poles love eating sunflower seeds. The seeds and the flowers are often the subject of Polish art, folk songs, and verse.

A History of Poland

An ancient land, Poland's flat plains stretch between Germany and Russia. This geographic location, with no natural borders, has determined much of its fate through the centuries.

Although archaeologists have found traces of human settlements near modern-day Kraków that date back 18,000 years, remains of village life near Biskupin are about 2,700 years old. It is here that Polish history really began.

Piast Poland

A legend of three brothers—Lech, Czech, and Rus—describes the founding of Poland. They were the leaders of an ancient Slavic tribe living in what is now Poland. Lech observed an eagle in a tree and took it as an omen to remain in Poland. Czech moved on to the lands of Bohemia. Rus moved east to Russia.

Poland's written history begins in 966 CE. When Prince Mieszko (myesh-kō) of the Piast Dynasty converted to Christianity, it led to the establishment of Roman Catholicism as the major faith. It united Poland with the development of Western Europe.

Under Kazimierz the Great—the last ruler of the Piast Dynasty—Poland expanded and grew in military strength, formed its legal and monetary systems, and founded the University of Kraków in 1364. The reign of Kazimierz was peaceful and prosperous. The Piasts ruled until 1370.

Jagiellonian Poland

In 1370, Jadwiga (yad-vēga), the niece of Kazimierz, became queen. She married Jagiello (ya-gyell-ō), a Lithuanian prince. This marriage created the Poland-Lithuanian commonwealth that expanded Poland's boundaries and military might. Although Jadwiga died in childbirth at age 25, the Jagiellonian dynasty ruled until 1572.

The Golden Age

The period from 1400 to the 1600 is known as Poland's Golden Age in architecture, science, and the arts. At the time of Christopher Columbus's first voyage to America in 1492, Poland was one of the largest and most powerful kingdoms in Europe, with territory from the Baltic to the Black Sea. Poland was also a multinational state that was a haven for Jews and people fleeing from the Spanish Inquisition.

During the Renaissance, Poland was known for protecting freedom of expression and encouraging the arts and learning. At this time, for example, Copernicus was studying astronomy and working on his theories that identified the sun and not the Earth as the center of the solar system

Copernicus

Nobles and Neighbors

In the constitution of 1505, the *szlachta* (shlok-ta) (the wealthy landowners) gained a large share of power and responsibility in government through the new *Sejm* (sāme) (the Parliament). Polish nobles grew in influence and elected Poland's kings for more than 200 years. The 16th and 17th centuries were a time of war with Poland's neighbors—Russia, Turkey, and Sweden.

In 1683, the Polish King Jan Sobieski, whom the nobles had elected, saved Europe from conquest by the Ottoman Turks at the Battle of Vienna. He was a hero, but the wars he fought were costly and ruined the Polish economy. In response to the Polish people's dissatisfaction with the king, they established the *liberum veto*, which gave each noble the right to veto legislation in Parliament. However, this privilege led to dissension among the nobles. A weak and splintered Poland was easy prey for its stronger neighbors. In 1772, Russia, Prussia, and Austria divided Poland for the first time.

The Polish Constitution

To reform and strengthen policies in Poland, the Constitution of May 3, 1791, included many features taken from the U.S. Constitution. It provided increased voting rights for the people and government reforms that included an end to *liberum veto*.

Poland's neighbors preferred a weak, splintered Poland; they objected to the Constitution and other reforms. Thus, Russia, Prussia, and Austria partitioned Poland twice more in 1793 and 1795. For 123 years, Poland did not exist as an independent country.

Tadeusz Kościuszko

Poles continued their struggle for freedom with armed resistance. Polish military leaders Tadeusz Kościuszko (kos-chūsh-ka) and Kazimierz Pułaski (pu-was-ki) fought for Polish freedom and later fought bravely in the American Revolutionary War. Pułaski even saved the life of General George Washington!

World War I

After World War I, Poland became a reunited independent country, as stipulated in President Woodrow Wilson's Fourteen Points—a speech he gave to the U.S. Congress in 1918 about the purpose of the War. In the 1920s and 1930s, Józef Piłsudski (pēw-sud-skē)- became the leader of Poland. He had mixed success with reforms and making the economy better. In 1925, Piłsudski overthrew the old government and set up a new one with more executive power. International economic inflation, the rise of Nazi Germany, and the threat of Stalin's Russia added to the pressures on the new state.

World War II

Kazimierz Pułaski

Poland was an independent country until German troops invaded it from the west on September 1, 1939. German dictator Adolph Hitler planned to crush all opposition to Germany during World War II and eventually annex parts of Poland for living space and agriculture.

This marked the beginning of World War II and the beginning of Poland's long nightmare. On September 17, 1939, Soviet troops invaded the country from the east. Poles were caught between the two invaders.

From 1939 to 1941, the Soviets deported more than 1 million Poles to Siberia. The Polish army officers who were not captured by the Germans were put in Soviet prisons and camps. Some 15,000 Polish officers were executed.

The Nazis occupied Poland for six years. The war years nearly destroyed the country. Six million people (one-fifth of the population) were killed, including 3 million Jews. The Nazis had their worst concentration camps on Polish soil. By the end of World War II, nearly all of the million people living in Warsaw had been killed or expelled from the country.

Post-War Poland

Poland's post-war fate was decided at the Yalta Conference in 1945 by Winston Churchill (Prime Minister of England), Franklin Delano Roosevelt (America's President), and Joseph Stalin (Premier of the Soviet Union). Poland became a Soviet *satellite*—that is, it was under Soviet political and economic control. Under the Polish Communist leader Wladyslaw (Vlad-ē-slav) Gomulka, a "Polish Road to Socialism" allowed for private ownership of farms. It also expanded freedom of speech and travel and tolerated the Roman Catholic Church.

This balancing act between Soviet control and independent home rule continued until economic and political conditions deteriorated badly. By 1970, life in Poland was extremely difficult. Food price increases led to protests. Workers' strikes and demonstrations brought a new leader, Edward Gierek, who instituted reforms and negotiated with workers.

Strikes and Solidarity

Gierek's reforms did not put an end to the workers' discontent. In 1980, another wave of strikes occurred in the Gdansk shipyards over low wages and rising food prices. This led to the establishment of Solidarity, an independent trade union headed by Lech Wałesa (va-wāsa). It also led to the anti-Communist movement.

Solidarity gained strength and inspiration from Polish Pope John-Paul II, who openly supported the Solidarity movement. Workers began to demand higher wages and improved working conditions and to challenge the authority of Communist leadership.

Concerned about further discontent, Poland's Marxist government was forced to recognize an independent union of workers. A nationwide strike followed. It led to a new government. Martial law (emergency rule led by the military) followed, along with the arrest of Lech Wałesa and others. In 1983, Wałesa won the Nobel Peace Prize. Martial law was lifted in 1984.

Lech Wałesa is welcomed in Krakow after a settlement between strikers and the government was announced.

By 1988, the poor economy led to new strikes, and the government allowed Solidarity to compete in the elections. Solidarity won, and Lech Wałesa was elected President in 1990. Free parliamentary elections followed in 1991. Poland now had Eastern Europe's first post-Communist government. It was no longer a Soviet satellite country.

Poland Today

During the 1990s, Poland managed to improve its economy. There are still many people making their living by farming. Poverty in the country is widespread. The unemployment rate is high, and younger Poles are leaving for employment in wealthier countries.

Nevertheless, living standards are rising. Foreign firms are investing in the country. Modernization, like the development of new shopping malls, is taking place. Infrastructure is being repaired. And many tourists from all over the world are beginning to discover its beautiful national parks and cultural attractions.

Its transformation to a democratic market economy is nearly complete. It is increasingly active in Euro-Atlantic organizations. Poland joined NATO in 1999 and the European Union in 2004. In 2003, during the Iraq War, a Polish-led international force that included 2,500 Polish troops took on peacekeeping responsibilities in south-central Iraq. Polish troops were withdrawn from Iraq in 2008.

Despite the incredible turmoil Poland has gone through, it maintains its distinct language and culture—and Poles are incredibly proud of both! The internal peace that it has found at last is giving it the chance to move forward.

Daily Life

For centuries, Poland was an agricultural society, with most of the population living in rural areas as peasant farmers. During the partitioning of Poland, the town populations increased. Skilled craftspeople moved in to form entrepreneurial classes, along with Germans, Jews, Scandinavians, Dutch, and Scots—all of whom engaged in trading. After Poland was unified at the end of World Wars I and II, even more people moved into the Polish towns. Today, there is a significant urban population in Poland.

Poles have suffered great tragedy, particularly in the last 100 years. But they remain warm, generous, and kind—particularly to visitors. Their hospitality is amazing! If you visit Poland, expect to be offered lots of food, friendship, and discussion about politics and the world at large. Poles live in the present!

Life in the City

Many Polish cities were destroyed during World War II. Since then, the rebuilding process has helped Polish cities modernize. The Old Town area of Warsaw has been beautifully reconstructed. The city is filled with cafes, clubs, and shops. It's as bustling as any big American city, yet you'll still see sights from the past, like peasant women selling flowers on the street.

Today, more than 60 percent of Poles live in urban areas. Many Poles live in high-rise apartment complexes called *bloki*, which were built after World War II. The apartments usually consist of three or four rooms.

Although many Poles in the cities now have cars, there are many inexpensive intercity trains and buses. Public transportation is popular and extremely crowded during rush hours.

Warsaw

In cities and towns all over Poland, you'll find lots of open-air markets selling everything from vegetables to counterfeit designer duds! The markets provide lots of opportunities for snapping up bargains. They also give people the chance to chat and enjoy the atmosphere. People who don't find what they're looking for in the market stalls can shop in the supermarkets and hypermarkets most towns and cities in Poland now have.

Life in the Country

More than 60 percent of the land is taken up by farming. Many of Poland's farm products are much in demand, such as fruits, vegetables, honey, hams, sausage, and dairy products. More than one-third of the Polish workforce works in agriculture. This only contributes about four percent to the country's Gross Domestic Product, however. Of the two million private farms in Poland, most are very small; they're often made up of separate pieces of land spread over a larger area.

Many people still cling to the old traditions and prefer to do things the way they've been done for years. You'll still see horse-drawn carts taking hay and crops from the fields. The farming families have a deep commitment to their land and animals, and to their communities—even if they don't make much money. Some Polish farming families supplement their income by taking paying guests into the farmhouse or in a separate building on the farm.

The farms of those who do make a good living are relatively small. About 200,000 farmers have plots of about 37 acres; 24,000 have plots of up to about 495 acres each. (Compare this to an average farm of the 1,000 or so acres needed to be successful.) Large-scale factory farms are not common.

The Family Unit

Poles highly value family life. Even younger people who are becoming more Westernized and independent have a strong commitment to their families. This means celebrating holidays together, spending time together, and honoring parents and relatives. Grandparents and grandkids enjoy an especially strong bond. There may be several generations of a family living under one roof. Adults may live close to their parents and stay in constant touch, visiting and helping out often.

What's in a Name?

Polish last names are generally passed down from the father to his children from generation to generation. A married woman generally takes her husband's last name. However, she can legally keep her maiden name (Smith) or add her husband's name to hers to create a double last name (Smith-Jones). It's possible (but rare) for a husband to adopt his wife's last name or to add her name to his family name.

Going to School

Poland has a long, rich tradition in education. After World War II, the government began providing free education. The literacy rate is now 99.8 percent.

All children between the ages of six and 18 attend school. Children in elementary grades walk to school; older kids take the bus or tram.

School is formal and demanding. The children study many subjects and do a lot of homework. Polish students often begin taking algebra classes and studying at least one foreign language in grade 6.

Polish students attend school six days a week, but they attend fewer hours each day than kids in the United States. In the first few grades, Polish students have the same teacher all day. In many schools, the kids wear slippers and smocks as part of their standard school uniform. They may also have small chores, such as cleaning chalkboards. When the teacher enters the room, Polish children stand and greet them with "Good day, Sir!" or "Good Day, Madam!"

Poland's Most Famous Son and Daughter

Pope John Paul II

Poland's most famous son was Pope John Paul II (1920–2005). You will see his picture proudly displayed in many homes, restaurants, and other places in Poland today.

He was born Karol Jozef Wojtyla (voy-too-a) in 1920, in southern Poland. After serving as priest, bishop, and cardinal for many years, he was elected Pope of the Roman Catholic Church in 1978. At age 58, he was the youngest pope since 1846; he was the first non-Italian pope since the 16th century.

From his earliest years as Pope, John Paul II openly opposed Communism. People credit him as one of the major forces that brought about the fall of the Soviet Union.

John Paul II maintained very conservative views on many issues, including divorce, stem cell research, human cloning, and euthanasia. Many in the Western world have criticized him for being too conservative. He is extremely popular in Poland to this day, however, and respected by Christians and non-Christians alike around the world.

After his death in 2005, many people (particularly Poles) demanded that he be made a saint. The campaign to accomplish this continues. He is often referred to as Pope John Paul II the Great.

Marie Curie

Marie Skłodowska (skwa-dov-ska) Curie (1867–1934) was a Polish physicist and chemist who never lost her devotion to Poland. She was a pioneer in the field of radioactivity and the first person to receive two Nobel Prizes.

Curie was born in Warsaw and lived there until age 24, when she went to study in Paris. She founded the Curie Institutes in Paris and Warsaw. Members of her family—her husband Pierre, her daughter Irène Joliot-Curie, and her son-in-law Frédéric Joliot-Curie—also received Nobel Prizes.

Her greatest achievements were developing a theory of radioactivity, techniques for isolating radioactive isotopes (atoms), and discovering polonium and radium (two new elements). Under Marie Curie, the world's first studies into the treatment of cancer using radioactive isotopes were conducted. Cancer is still treated with radiation today.

Language & Expressions

Here are some fun facts about verbal and nonverbal communication in Poland.

Famous Polish Proverbs

Here are ten famous Polish proverbs. What do you think they mean?

When a person is in a hurry, the devil is happy.
Every penny adds up.
You rest the way you have made your bed.
When among the crows, caw as the crows do.
Everywhere is fine, but best at home.
All times are good when you are old.
Do not push the river; it will flow by itself.
The greatest oaks have been little acorns.
Wherever you go, you can't get rid of yourself.
It's better to have a sparrow in your hand than a pigeon on the roof.

Body Language and Etiquette in Poland

Here are some examples of body language and etiquette you'll find in Poland.

Do not chew gum while you are speaking.

Men may greet women by kissing their hands.

Women greet other women with a slight hug and kiss on the check.

Maintain eye contact and smile when you are being introduced to someone.

If invited to someone's house, bring flowers or a small gift. The next day, write a thank-you note.

Say, "Hello," "Good-bye," and "Thank you" when entering and leaving stores, hotels, and restaurants.

It is considered impolite not to leave a tip in restaurants or with cab drivers.

In some parts of Poland, guests are expected to remove their shoes before entering the host's home. In other parts of Poland, removing the shoes might be considered offensive. Take a cue from the host. If the host is wearing shoes, keep yours on. If the host is not wearing shoes, remove yours and leave them outside the door.

Many Polish people use a lot of hand gestures when they talk.

Sitting with your ankle resting on your knee or standing with your hands in your pockets is viewed as disrespectful.

Know before You Go

Here are some common phrases you will use in Poland. The spelling and pronunciation are also given. Try them out! Look up some additional ones!

English	**Polish**	**Pronunciation**
Yes/No	Tak/Nie	Tahk/Nye
Mr./Mrs.	Pan/Pani	Pahn/Pahn–ee
Good day, or Good morning	Dzień dobry	Dzhehn DOHB–ree
Good evening	Dobry wieczór	Dohb–ree VYEH–choor
Good night	Dobranoc	Doh–BRA.H–nohts
Goodbye	Do widzenia	Doh vee–DZEHN–yah
Good	Dobrze	DOB–zheh
How are you?	Jak się masz?	Yahk SHEH mahsh
Thank you!	Dziękuję	Dzhen–KOO–ye
Welcome!	Witamy!	Vee–tah–mee
Please, You're welcome.	Proszę	Pro–SHEH
Excuse me.	Przepraszam	Pshe–pra–sham.

Numbers

1	Jeden	YEH–den
2	Dwa	Dvah
3	Trzy	Tchee
4	Cztery	Chteh–ree
5	Pięć	Pyench
6	Sześć	Shayshch
7	Siedem	Shyeh–dem.
8	Osiem	Oh–shyem.
9	Dziewięć	Dzhyeh–vyehnch
10	Dziesięć	Dzhyeh–shehnch

Name _____   Date _____

MATCH THE POLISH AND ENGLISH WORDS

Polish has many words that are close to words in English. Read the simple Polish words in the left-hand column. Draw a line to the same word in English in the right-hand column.

1. KALKULATOR
2. PARK
3. PREZENT
4. CZEKOLADA
5. ATLAS
6. MAPA
7. KLASA
8. GLOBUS
9. BANK
10. RADIO
11. TELEWIZJA
12. LAMPA
13. PIANINO
14. KOMPUTER

A. CHOCOLATE
B. MAP
C. GLOBE
D. RADIO
E. LAMP
F. PIANO
G. CALCULATOR
H. COMPUTER
I. CLASS
J. PRESENT
K. BANK
L. ATLAS
M. TELEVISION
N. PARK

FOODS

Welcome to Polish Cooking

Poles are known for their hospitality, and an important part of Polish hospitality is providing large quantities of food. Polish food is delicious! It's well-seasoned and, as some would say, 'it's hearty comfort food that hits the spot!"

Vegetables and grains, like wheat and barley, are staples of the Polish diet. Bread is served at every meal. If you like pickled vegetables, you'll get lots of them in Poland: pickled cucumbers, beet, and cabbage all play a big part in Polish cooking. Poland's beautiful forests are filled with wild mushrooms, which are put into lots of recipes. Sour cream tops lots of dishes.

Meat (especially pork) is definitely the star of most meals. Kielbasa, the tasty Polish sausage, is a staple of Polish cuisine. More than 1,000 kinds of kielbasa are made in Poland.

Common Foods

Pierogi

Eaten as a snack or as a main course for lunch or dinner, pierogis are the cornerstone of Polish cooking. These small, half-moon-shaped pockets of dough are stuffed with delicious fillings, such as potato, cottage cheese, cabbage, ground beef, or even berries. They're usually boiled and served with fried onions (except for fruit pierogis). They can also be baked or fried and topped with a dollop of sour cream or garlic sauce and bacon bits.

pierogi

Placki

Potato pancakes, or placki, are another Polish favorite found on everyone's table. They are often cooked with mushrooms or smoked meat. You wouldn't soon forget the taste of placki!

Soups

Soups are a cornerstone of the Polish diet. *Bigos* is known in English as hunter's stew, and everyone has their own favorite recipe for it. It is made from cabbage, meat, and mushrooms. This savory soup is so hearty it's really more of a main course that could satisfy even the biggest appetite.

Zurek is a rye broth that is seasoned with dill and served with sausage and egg. *Barszcz* (barsht) is a clear, red beet soup, often served with a little pastry on the side. Other common soups at the Polish table are chicken, barley, potato, tomato, mushroom, and vegetable.

Snacks

If you're looking for snack foods, you'll find McDonald's®, KFC®, and Pizza Hut®. Pizza is especially common. You'll find it in cities and towns all over Poland.

Zapiekanka is a common, low-cost snack food. It's one-half of a long baguette topped with mushrooms, meat, cheese, vegetables, or even pineapple. It's served baked.

Daily Meals

Breakfast in Poland, as with other places in Europe, is light. People might have a cup of tea or coffee and a roll.

Lunch and dinner are much heavier meals. They generally begin with a cold appetizer like herring in sour cream with onions or paté (chopped liver). Hot appetizers can include pierogies or a piece of kielbasa. After the appetizer, a bowl of soup is served.

Main courses consist of meat (chicken, pork, beef, or even game meat like venison) and fish. Side dishes are usually made of potatoes.

Desserts include fruit pierogies, ice cream, thin pancakes filled with jam or cheese, cookies, and pastries made with poppy seeds. Berries (strawberries, cherries, and blueberries) are served fresh, stewed with sour cream or made into jams.

The entire meal will probably be washed down with tea, which Poles usually drink in a glass with sugar. Coffee might be served, but it isn't nearly as popular as tea.

Holidays & Festivals

The Easter Season

Fat Thursday

On the Thursday before Ash Wednesday, which begins the fasting of the Easter season, Poles eat lots of jelly donuts called *paczki* (pounch-kē). This custom stems from the need to use up fats, eggs, and dairy products before the fasting of the Lenten season begins. People make the most of it by eating several of these sweet treats throughout the day.

Easter

Easter is celebrated with feasting. On Holy Saturday, the day before Easter, families fill baskets with *pisanki* (colored eggs) and food and take the basket to church to be blessed.

At home, the Easter table is set with a traditional sugar lamb in the center of it. There is also sausage, ham, veal, pork, pound cake, cheesecakes, and many other savory dishes. Colorful decorated eggs are placed together with bread and salt, the traditional symbols of hospitality. Cheese cakes and *baba* (sweet yeast cakes) cover the table. Family members and guests exchange wishes of good health and good fortune and share a piece of hard-boiled egg that has been blessed. On Easter, anyone can visit another home without having an invitation, since everyone who owns a home holds an open house.

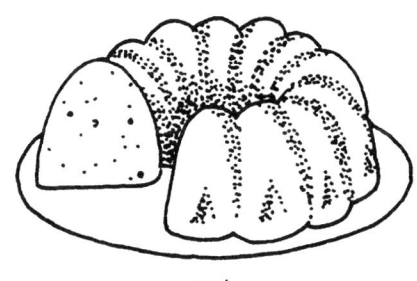

Baba

Śmigus-Dyngus

On Easter Monday, during a holiday called Śmigus-Dyngus (or Wet Monday), boys run around the villages, towns, and cities throwing water on people. According to tradition, girls who get soaked with water will marry within the year.

Polish Constitution Day • *May 3*

Poles all around the globe celebrate Polish Constitution Day, which is one of the main national holidays in the country. Ceremonies, marches, concerts, and other festivities mark the happy occasion of May 3, 1791, the anniversary of the passage of Poland's first constitution.

All Saints' Day • *November 1*

This special day, also called Day of the Dead, honors all of those who have died. Poles take flowers (especially autumn flowers like chrysanthemums), wreaths, and candles to the cemeteries to honor family, friends, and national heroes. Poles believe that their prayers and candles will help the departed souls. All Polish cemeteries glow with the flickering candles in the evening as people celebrate and attend church services.

Polish Independence Day • *November 11*

One of the main national holidays in Poland, Independence Day marks the anniversary of the restoration of Polish independence in 1918. As with Constitution Day, ceremonies, marches, concerts, and other festivities mark this patriotic holiday.

The Christmas Season • *December 24 to February 2*

Christmas is a magical time in Poland, starting with a beautiful Christmas tree decorated with *piernik* (honey cookies) made in the shape of toys or animals.

Christmas Eve is the most widely celebrated holiday in Poland. It is believed that how Christmas Eve is spent affects the coming year. Thus, it is to be spent peacefully with family. The Christmas Eve dinner is the center of the family observance; all preparations for the dinner are to be done before sundown. Traditionally, the dinner has twelve courses (to reflect the twelve months of the coming year). The meatless menu consists of fish, soup, vegetables, and sweets. *Kutia* is a special dessert of wheat grains, poppy seeds, honey, and almonds.

The whole family sits down to dine when the first star appears in the sky. An extra place is set to welcome unexpected guests. Sheaves of wheat and rye are placed in the corners of the room. Hay is placed under the tablecloth to remind guests of the manger where Christ was born. Some people also put money, a fish scale, or a fish bone into a wallet to ensure prosperity in the coming year.

Before dinner, the head of the family divides a special wafer called *opłatek* (op-wa-tek) that symbolizes love and friendship among family and friends. This sharing is so important that the opłatek is mailed to those who are not present. The head of the household goes to the barn after dinner to give a special treat, including pink opłatek, to the animals. According to Polish folklore, animals can talk on Christmas Eve.

Gifts are given on Christmas Eve after the family sings Christmas carols. In the countryside, carolers go from house to house with a lighted star on a stick. As they sing, they receive candy and other holiday treats.

Name Day

Most Polish kids over the age of 13 celebrate their Name Day rather than a birthday. Since religion plays such an important part in Poles' daily life, Polish children are traditionally named after saints. In the Roman Catholic Church, each day of the year is designated as the feast day of one or more saints. Thus, kids celebrate the feast day of the saint for whom they were named. They receive small gifts like flowers and chocolates.

Polish Weddings

Polish weddings are known throughout the world for being happy, long celebrations! After the church ceremony, the reception will go on for hours (or days).

In Poland, it is traditional for the bride to cry during the wedding. If she doesn't, legend has it that she will cry throughout her married life. At the reception, the parents of the bride and groom greet the newly married couple. They offer them bread (sprinkled with salt for protection) so they will never hunger and a goblet of wine so they will never be thirsty. The bride and groom taste the bread and wine, then break the glass and plate for good luck. The parents kiss the bride and groom to show their love and unity. Then, the feasting begins!

Polish weddings in the smaller villages typically have many more guests because the villagers usually have their own homes and can accommodate more guests. Village weddings can last up to three days! People living in city apartments have smaller places and can't invite as many guests.

The day after the wedding, there is usually a party at the home of the bride's or groom's parents. Everyone enjoys the leftover food and drink from the wedding.

Festivals

Religious Festivals

Poland is a predominantly Roman Catholic country, and Christian ceremonies and processions are common, especially during the Christmas and Easter seasons. People also make pilgrimages to holy sites.

There are countless roadside shrines throughout Poland, found in places like the entrance to a village or at a major crossroads. Poles particularly honor Mary, the mother of Jesus. Many smaller shrines dedicated to her are scattered throughout the country.

Harvest Festivals

From mid-August to early September, harvest festivals take place all over Poland. People celebrate by dancing, singing, sampling local foods, and dressing in original costumes. A major feature of each festival is the harvest wreath, made from corn, wheat, rye, and flowers. In some parts of Poland, local villages compete with each other to see who can make the best harvest wreaths.

Creative Arts

Music and Dance

Poles have a rich tradition of regional folk songs and dances. Polish folk dances vary from the brisk Oberek, Mazurek, and Krakowiak (krak-ō-vē-ak), to the courtly Polonaise. Several folk dance troupes, including Mazowsze (ma-zov-sha) and Śląsk, have toured internationally and are famous worldwide.

Poland now has folk music festivals that feature dancing in folk costume. Sometimes, groups compete against one another, with experts in traditional folk music, dance, and costume judging their performances.

Folk Costumes

Each region of Poland has its own traditional folk costumes that are still worn for special occasions, such as weddings. They are brightly colored; decorated with embroidery; and can include aprons, vests, and ribbons. Beautiful headdresses include hats and wreaths of flowers.

Costumes from the Kraków area

The Polka

Think of Polish music *and* dance, and the polka probably comes to mind. Ironically, you won't hear the polka much in Poland today, but it's one of the first things we think of when we think of Polish music and dance.

The lively polka is of Czechoslovakian origin and probably got its name from the Czech word for *half*. This refers to the half-step of the dance. In Polish, the word *polka* means Polish woman.

In the 1830s, the polka spread across Europe and became a major dance craze! American First Lady Julia Tyler, wife of President John Tyler, introduced it to the White House in the 1840s. The polka was so popular during this time that it became attached to lots of things that had nothing to do with dancing, like hats, fans, cakes, and hairstyles. The symmetrical dots on a new fabric, for instance, were called *polka dots*. We still use the term today.

Frédéric Chopin: Poland's Great Composer

Frédéric Chopin (1810–1849) was a master of Romantic music and Poland's greatest composer. He was a child prodigy on the piano and was giving concerts and composing complex music by the age of seven. Lots of people have compared his talent to Wolfgang Amadeus Mozart's abilities.

Chopin was an extremely successful composer and performer, and he influenced many other great composers. His nocturnes, waltzes, preludes, and other works are emotional and highly memorable. His Mazurkas and Polonaise dances reflect Polish folk themes.

Folk Art

The many Polish folk arts and crafts reflect the country's early agricultural society.

Wycinanki

Wycinanki (vē-chē-nan-kē) (cuts of paper) are intricate Polish paper cut-outs that developed in the 19th century. They resemble delicate snowflakes cut from colored paper. They were once used to decorate the walls and ceiling beams of country cottages. Today they are highly prized by folk art collectors. The flowers, stars, peacocks, roosters, and decorative scenes showing special events reflect a high level of skill. This folk art has been passed down through the generations.

Wooden Plates, Boxes, and Easter Eggs

Locals and tourists alike love Poland's decorative carved wooden plates and boxes. These beautiful pieces were made by farmers and shepherds in Poland's Tatra Mountains who carved Linden wood during the long winter months centuries ago.

Today, Polish folk artists use the same techniques and materials. They burn outlines of patterns into the wood surface of the plate or box. Then they hand-color each piece with wood stain or paint. The pieces might also be inlaid with brass or copper to add sparkle. Nested plates and boxes, in which smaller pieces are nested inside or on top of larger ones, are popular.

Wood-carved nested eggs are an extremely popular Polish folk art, too. The eggs are hand-carved and hand-painted, usually with floral motifs.

Polish Amber

Poland probably sells more amber than any other country in Europe. You will see amber sculptures and jewelry in expensive galleries, retail shops, and street vendor carts. Amber, which is a golden orange color, is fossilized tree resin. It is not a mineral, but it is often referred to as a gemstone. Amber can sometimes contain insects or even tiny vertebrates.

There are many folk tales associated with amber and its healing effects. Some people think that wearing amber has a strong and positive effect on the body. For example, amber necklaces are said to have a healing effect on illnesses of the thyroid and swelling in the neck.

Polish Pottery

Polish pottery produced in the town of Boleslawiec (bol-a-swav-yets) in southwestern Poland is some of the finest pottery in the world. Once you've seen this beautiful pottery, you'll never forget it!

These thick stoneware pieces are hand-formed from opaque white clay. Then they are hand-painted in intricate designs with small stamps soaked in brightly colored paint. The decorative themes used on the pottery number in the thousands.

You can find Polish pottery in some of the best gift and kitchenware shops. Regardless of the design on each piece, all of the pieces seem to go together. A table set with Polish pottery or accented with Polish pottery serving pieces is a cheerful sight!

Name _____   Date _____

MAKE A WYCINANKI

Materials Needed
- white sheet of paper
- colored sheet of construction paper
- scissors
- glue

Directions
1. Fold your piece of white paper.
2. Find a Wycinanki pattern using the Internet or another resource. You can also come up with some of your own!
3. Place your pattern on the fold. Trace the outline of the pattern on your paper.
4. Cut around your pencil outline.
5. Unfold your white piece of paper. The remaining paper is your Wycinanki.
6. Glue your finished white Wycinanki onto a piece of colored construction paper.

Sports & Games

Football

Polish kids love to play football (soccer). It's also one of the most popular spectator sports in the country. Poles are no strangers to international soccer competitions. The Polish national football team finished third in the 1974 and 1982 FIFA (Federation International of Football Association) World Cup competitions. The team won a gold medal at the 1972 Summer Olympic Games and silver medals at the Games in 1976 and 1992.

Other Sports

Kids and adults alike enjoy volleyball, basketball, hockey, ping-pong, fencing, and weightlifting. The Polish men's volleyball team is ranked seventh in the world; the women's team is ranked ninth.

The Polish mountains are ideal for hiking, skiing, and biking. The beaches are ideal for lots of water sports like swimming, fishing, canoeing, and kayaking.

Play Polish Games

"Everything with Feathers Flies"

Number of Players Needed
5 to 10

Materials Needed
- Table large enough for all players to sit around it
- Chairs for each player

Directions
1. Choose a leader to start.
2. The leader calls out the name of an animal.
3. If the animal has feathers, the other players hit the table and repeat the name of the animal.
4. If someone hits the table when an animal without feathers is called out, that player is eliminated.
5. The last person left is the winner and becomes the leader of the next game.

"Salonowiec" (sa-lō-nō-vē-est)

Number of Players Needed
3 to 7

Materials Needed
A flat surface to lean against (like a fence, wall, or tree)

Directions
1. Choose a person to start the game.
2. This person turns his or her back, leans on the flat surface, and closes his or her eyes.
3. All the other players crowd behind the person.
4. One of the players taps the chosen person on the back.
5. The chosen person turns around and tries to guess who tapped him or her.
6. If the chosen person guesses correctly, whoever tapped him or her takes the person's place.
7. If the next person does not guess who tapped him or her, all of the players tap the person, one at a time, until the chosen player guesses correctly.

"The Old Bear"

Number of Players Needed
5 to 10 or more

Materials Needed
Large room

Directions
1. Choose one person as the bear. Have the bear sit in the middle of a circle, pretending to be asleep and snoring loudly.

2. Everyone else holds hands, walks in a circle around the bear, and either says or sings these words:

   Old bear is sleeping deeply,
   Old bear is sleeping deeply,
   We walked on our tiptoes as we're afraid of him,
   When he'd wake up he would eat us!
   When he'd wake up he would eat us!

3. Then, everyone stands still in the circle and recites:
   The first hour (passed). The bear sleeps.
   The second hour (passed). The bear snores.
   The third hour...the bear wakes up and he's catching us!!!

3. Then the bear stands up and tries to catch somebody while everyone breaks the circle and runs away, trying to escape.

4. The caught person is a new bear, and the game repeats.

Poland – MP5126

ROMANIA

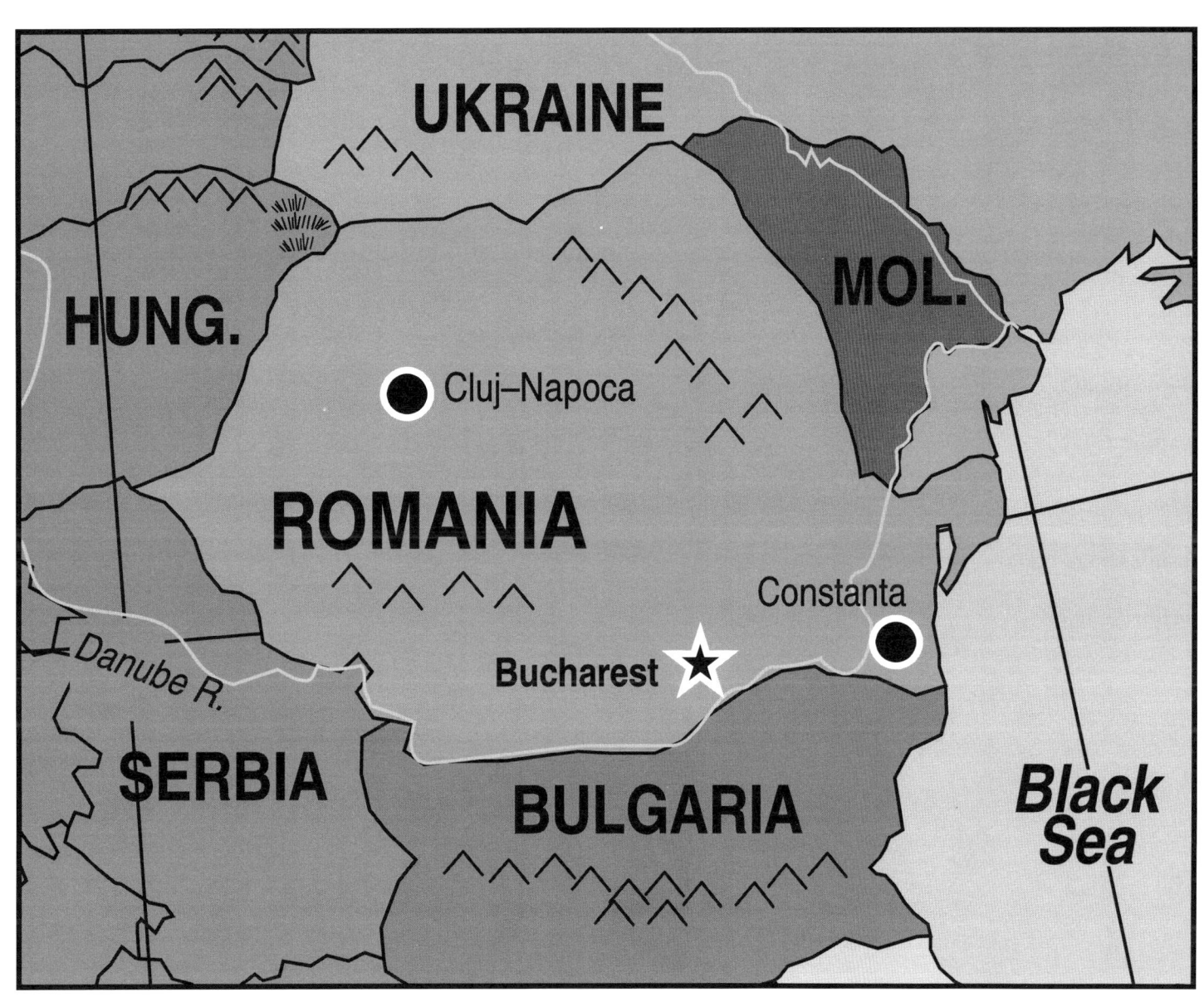

WELCOME TO ROMANIA!

Romania is famous for being home to the vampire Dracula, but this country is so much more than a fictional character! No longer in the shadow of its Communist past, it is one of Europe's fastest-growing economies. Since joining the European Union (EU) in 2007, Romania is becoming Westernized like its former Soviet neighbors. But its charming mountain villages and medieval castles assure its fairy tale charm. Wherever you land in Romania, there is something old and something new—and a whole lot of hospitality, history, and culture that unite the two.

FAST FACTS

Official Name: Romania

Location: Southeastern Europe, bordering the Black Sea. Romania is between Bulgaria on the south and Ukraine on the north and the east. Serbia is to the southwest, Hungary is to the northwest, and Moldova to the northeast.

Population: 22,181,287 (2010 estimate)

Capital City: Bucharest

Area: 92,043 square miles; Romania is slightly smaller than the state of Oregon.

Major Language: Romanian

Major Religions: Eastern Orthodox: 86.8%
Protestant: 7.5%
Roman Catholic: 4.7%

Currency: The leu (which means *lion*)   1 leu = 100 bani

Climate: Temperate; Romania has cold, cloudy winters with frequent snow and fog, and sunny summers with frequent showers and thunderstorms.

The Land: The Central Transylvanian Basin is separated from the Moldavian Plateau on the east by the Eastern Carpathian Mountains and separated from the Wallachian Plain on the south by the Transylvanian Alps.

Type of Government: Republic

Flag: From the hoist side, three equal vertical bands of blue, yellow, and red. The government hasn't assigned an official meaning to the colors, but the present colors were used by various revolutions and movements of the 19th century.

Coat of Arms:	A golden eagle is the central image of Romania's Coat of Arms. The eagle holds a cross in its beak and a mace (a ceremonial rod) and a sword in each claw. The arms are red, yellow, and blue—the colors of the Romanian flag.
National Flower:	Dog rose (Rosa canina)
National Animal:	Golden eagle
Motto:	"Nothing without God" "All in One"

Natural Environment

Think of the setting for a fairly tale, with deep, dark woods, blue skies, and snow-capped mountains. You've just pictured Romania!

Romania's spectacular beauty comes from its natural environment of mountains, hills, and plains—much of which have not been developed. About half of the country is covered with ecosystems—natural and semi-natural areas like wetlands and forests. Almost half of the Romanian forest is undisturbed, thanks to the country's extensive conservation efforts.

Mountains and Regions

Of all the things that Romania is known for, the Carpathian Mountains are at the top of the list. Many of Romania's important cities and towns are located there.

The Carpathians extend about 600 miles through the center of the country. The mountains are low to medium altitude and about 60 miles across at their widest. Several major rivers run through them. The many summit passes of the Carpathians make them easier to cross than other European mountain ranges. There are also many relatively flat areas at high altitudes where lots of people live.

The Carpathians are divided into three ranges: the Eastern Carpathians, the Southern Carpathians (called the Transylvanian Alps), and the Western Carpathians.

The Eastern Carpathians have three ridges that run northwest to southeast. The ridge on the west is an extinct volcanic range with many depressions that contain important mining, industrial, and farming centers. They also contain important gold and silver deposits. About 32 percent of Romania's forests are found here, too. Tourists flock to this area to soak in the mineral springs at many of the health resorts.

The highest mountain peaks of the Carpathians are in the Transylvania Alps, which have more than 150 glacial lakes. You won't find the major depressions here that exist in the Eastern Carpathians. You will find grasslands and forests. At higher elevations, erosion has turned the rocks into spectacular figures that resemble famous monuments, such as the Sphinx in Egypt. These weathered rocks are popular tourist spots.

The Western Carpathians, which are the lowest of the three ranges, have deep depressions that once were used as gateways to other countries. The most famous of these is the Iron Gate on the Danube River, which forms part of the boundary between Serbia and Romania. There are more people here than in any other area of Romania. In the Apuseni Mountains, the northernmost area of the Western Carpathians, there are still many villages that exist at very high altitudes.

mania is divided into nine regions. The best known is the Transylvanian Plateau. This large, flat land is an important farming area that also contains large deposits of methane gas and salt. Tourists love its medieval castles and deep forests, set against the mountains. The area is growing rapidly. Today, you're likely to see modern shopping complexes and construction projects to further develop the area. People also think of Transylvania as the home of the fictional vampire Dracula. The real-life character who probably served as the model for Dracula—Vlad Tepes—was a 15th century prince of the southern Romanian region of Wallachia. Although he had brutal methods, Romanians still think of him as a savior who defended their country against cruel invaders. The capital of Bucharest is located in Wallachia.

Rivers

The Danube is the most important river in Romania. It travels about 40 percent of the country's entire length. Almost every river in Romania is a tributary of the Danube. These include the Mures, the Olt, the Prut, the Siret, the Ialomita, the Somes, and the Arges rivers. They primarily flow east, west, and south from the central Carpathians.

The Danube is the brightest gem in the crown of Romania's rivers. It's a major transportation route for goods being shipped within the country and to the world. It's also an important source of hydroelectric power. One of Europe's largest hydroelectric stations is located at the Iron Gate. The Danube Delta Reserve Biosphere, most of which is in Romania, is Europe's largest wetland. In 1991, more than 50 percent of this area was named a World Heritage Site.

Plants and Animals

The forests of Romania are filled with oak, ash, beech, spruce, fir, pine, and juniper trees. Beyond the forests are Alpine meadows filled with fragrant herbs.

With so much forestland in Romania, it's not surprising that forest-dwellers like bears, wolves, deer, lynxes, boars, foxes, woodpeckers, and eagles are found all over the country—especially bears. In fact, Romania has the world's largest population of wild bears. They even come down from the forests, searching neighborhoods for food. There are so many bears that campers are told to set up their tents in the open instead of under trees in order to avoid the bears!

In addition to these forest-dwellers, there are thousands of species of mammals, birds, fish, reptiles, and amphibians in Romania. The Carpathian chamois, a beautiful goat-antelope species, is the best known of these species.

Hundreds of species of birds inhabit the Danube Delta, such as pelicans, swans, wild geese, and flamingos—all of whom are protected by law. The delta is also a common stop for migrating birds.

Name _____ Date _____

THE REGIONS OF ROMANIA

Romania is divided into nine regions that are listed below. Using the Internet and other resources, find a map that shows the regions of Romania. Write the name of each region where it belongs on the map. Then write one or two words in each region that tell what it's known for.

- Banat
- Bucovina
- Crişana
- Dobrogea
- Maramureş
- Moldavia
- Oltenia
- Transylvania
- Wallachia

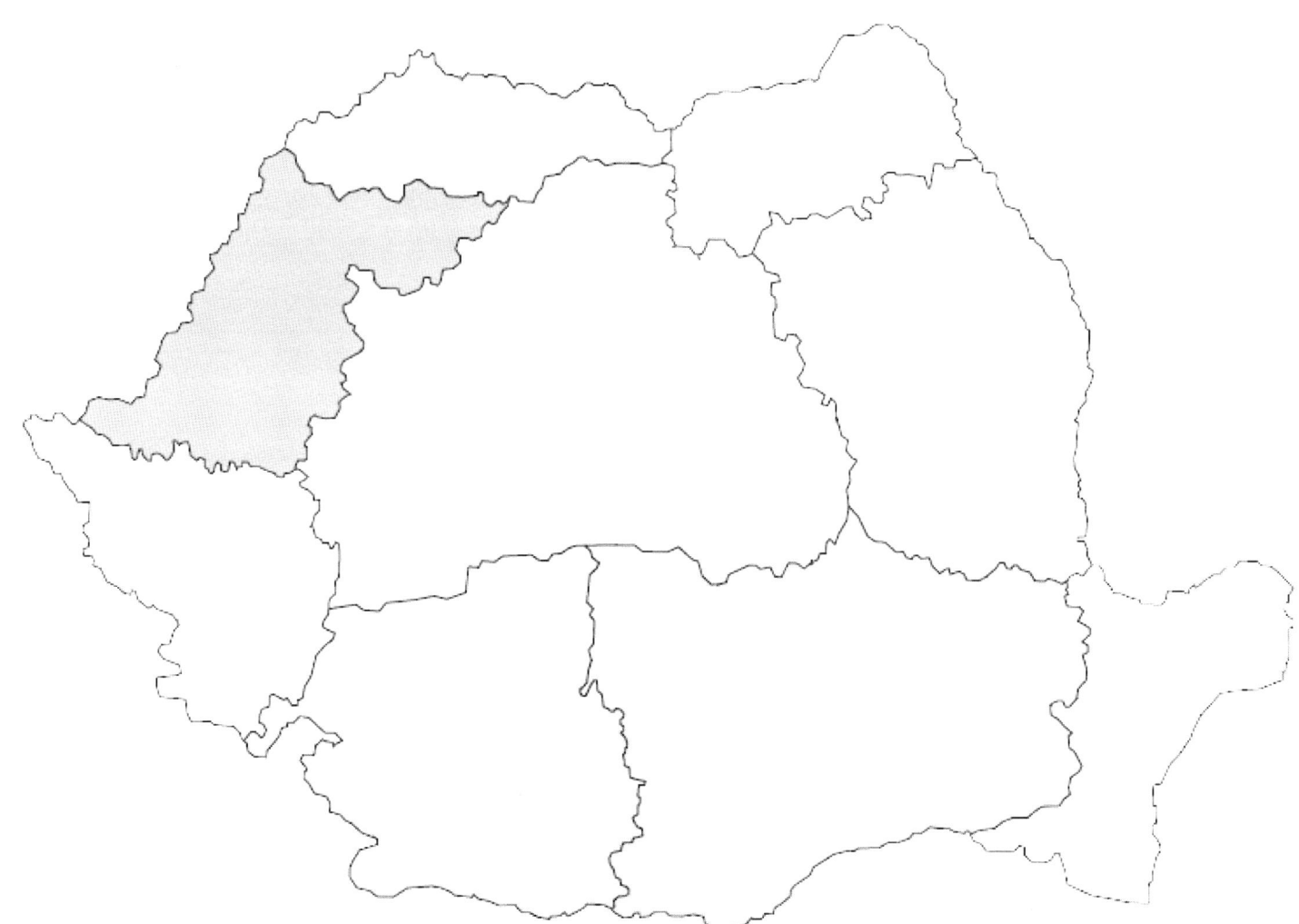

MP5126 – Romania

A History of Romania

Ancient Times

In ancient times, Romania was inhabited by tribes from Dacia, an area around the Carpathian Mountains that extended east to the Black Sea. The Dacian Kingdom was most powerful in the first century BCE. The network of forts and shrines the Dacians built in current southwestern Transylvania are now UNESCO World Heritage sites.

The Romans conquered the Dacians in 106 CE. Most of the Dacian lands became part of the Roman Empire (which is where the name *Romania* comes from). The Romans rapidly developed the area, which was rich in natural resources like gold. They built cities and roads (some ancient Roman roads still exist in the Carpathians). People from all over the Roman Empire came to live in the region. The Romans only ruled for about 200 years, but their influence is still strong in the culture and language of the Romanian people.

The Middle Ages

In the early Middle Ages, Hungarians began to settle in modern-day Transylvania, which eventually became part of the Kingdom of Hungary. As early as the 12th century CE, Germans also settled in the area.

To protect themselves from frequent invaders, such as the Turks, the people built well-fortified cities and castles, many of which still exist. The principalities of Wallachia and Moldavia were created in the 14th century. They fought hard against invaders from the Ottoman Empire, but both of them fell to it, starting in the 15th century. Also known as the Turkish Empire, the Ottoman Empire controlled much of Southeastern Europe, Western Asia, and North Africa at the height of its power in the 16th and 17th centuries.

An Independent Nation

In 1859, Wallachia and Moldavia were united, creating what we know as modern Romania. It was recognized as an independent nation in 1878.

World War I

When World War I broke out in 1914, Romania declared itself neutral. But in 1916, it joined the Allies and declared war on Austria-Hungary with the promise that it would receive several territories. Unfortunately, Romania was seriously unprepared for war, and its military campaign ended in disaster. Two-thirds of the country was conquered. Most of its army was captured or killed within four months.

Despite this devastation, Moldavia remained with Romania after the invaders were stopped in 1917. Austria-Hungary and the Russian Empire collapsed by 1917. Transylvania and Eastern Moldavia (which is present-day Moldova to the east of Romania) joined Romania in 1918.

The armistice signed in 1918 doubled Romania's size. It acquired vast land from Russia and the Austro-Hungarian Empire, including Bessarabia, Transylvania, and Bukovina. A Hungarian area called the Banat was divided with Yugoslavia.

King Carol II

King Carol II

King Carol II was crowned in 1930, but ruled more as a dictator than a monarch. In 1938, he abolished Romania's democratic constitution and banned the Iron Guard, which he had originally supported. (The Iron Guard was a Romanian political party that existed from 1927 into the early part of World War II. It was ultra-patriotic, supported fascism, and was against Jews.)

In 1940, Romania was reorganized as a fascist state. Despite King Carol's ban on the Iron Guard, it became the party in power. The Soviet Union occupied Bessarabia and northern Bukovina. King Carol II dissolved the Romanian parliament. He gave the new prime minister, Ion Antonescu, full power over the country, along with the Iron Guard. The king left his throne and went into exile. Antonescu became supreme leader.

World War II

Antonescu had been a Romanian soldier and a hero during World War I. Within months of taking over leadership of Romania, he crushed the Iron Guard. He also thrust the country into World War II by forming an alliance with Nazi Germany, Italy, and Japan. During the war, Romania was Nazi Germany's chief source of oil. Because of this, Romania was bombed heavily in an attempt to stop the oil production. With the Nazi invasion of the Soviet Union, Romania recovered Bessarabia and northern Bukovina from Soviet Russia.

Antonescu was responsible for the deaths of up to 450,000 or more people during the Holocaust, most of them Bessarabians, Ukrainian and Romanian Jews, and Romani Romanians. (The Romani are Romania's second largest ethnic minority after Hungarians.)

In 1944, Antonescu was arrested by Romania's King Michael I. Romania actually changed sides in World War II and joined the Allies in defeating Nazi Germany. But the cost to Romania was great. The Romanian army suffered several hundred thousand casualties in addition to the hundreds of thousands of people lost to the Holocaust.

Communist Romania

Romania was to experience more severe and difficult times after World War II. Soviet forces were still in the country, which led to a Communist government. In 1947, King Michael I was forced to leave his throne *and* leave the country. The monarchy was abolished. Romania was declared a Soviet people's republic. It remained under the control of the Soviet Union until the 1950s. The country's natural resources were drained. Far worse was the reign of terror carried out by the Romanian communist government well into the early 1960s.

The Secret Police launched several campaigns to eliminate "enemies of the state." Many people, from ordinary citizens to politicians and other officials, who spoke out against the government were killed, put in prisons or labor camps, or deported.

By 1965, Nicolae Ceauşescu (chow-ches-ko) had come to power. He was feared and hated throughout the country and world. Marshal Ceauşescu was not as enthusiastic toward the Soviet Union as former Romanian leaders had been. Under his dictatorship, he allowed the Secret Police greater power, and human rights abuses increased. The people lived in great poverty. He was eventually overthrown and executed in the Romanian Revolution of 1989. Romania was the only former Soviet country of Eastern Europe to overthrow its leader.

After Ceauşescu's death, former Communists dominated the Romanian government until 1996. They were swept from power and eventually replaced by the Social Democratic Party.

The 2004 elections brought to power an alliance formed by the National Liberal and Democratic parties. They currently govern the country. That same year, Romania joined NATO. It became a member country of the EU in 2007. As of 2008, Emil Boc is Prime Minister.

Romania Today

The Western world still knows little about Romania. Unfortunately, many people still see this beautiful, ancient, and historic land as dark and devastated. Nothing could be less true.

Even after its turbulent history, Romania is recovering remarkably well. As of 2009, the government began a three-year program of heavily upgrading the country's roads, factories, and railroad system. It still has a long way to go to reach the level of prosperity in Western Europe, but its membership in the EU will help boost its economy. Its main exports are electric machinery and equipment, textiles and footwear, mining, timber, construction materials, metals, chemicals, food processing, and petroleum refining.

WHAT DID THE ARCHAEOLOGISTS FIND?

Archaeologists in Romania are always finding new locations in which to dig relics from its ancient past. Below are scrambled names of some of the items they've uncovered. Unscramble the name of each object, and write them on the lines below.

1. T T E R Y O P _____

2. O O T L _____

3. E E L T C A B R _____

4. G N I R _____

5. K O H O _____

6. X A E _____

7. T T S A U E _____

8. N O P E W A _____

9. S T L E R N A _____

10. W P L O _____

11. H W E L E _____

12. E V O S T _____

13. N E O B _____

14. I O N S C _____

15. D L O G _____

MP5126 – Romania

Daily Life

Wherever you look in Romania, you'll find the very old contrasted with the very new—and some things in between. Go to a big city like Bucharest, and you'll see gray cement housing blocks from the Soviet days, medieval churches, brand new office buildings, lovely museums, traffic jams, peaceful parks, roads under construction, and lots of people grabbing a snack from street vendors—or from McDonalds®! Go to the countryside, and you'll find horse-drawn buggies, haystacks, shepherds with their sheep, and tourists zooming in new cars on unpaved roads that once only served wagons.

The Family Unit and Daily Life

The family is the key social unit in Romanian society. This includes immediate relatives, along with extended family such as aunts and uncles. Romanians are increasingly leading Westernized lives in which they move further from family for better opportunities, but the family still provides their primary social network. Family members also provide each other with money and other help in times of need.

The family unit remains traditional. The father is the head of the household. The mother, who may work outside the home, still takes care of the kids and does the household chores. Kids are expected to respect their parents and elders and help around the house.

Daily life on the whole, however, is probably pretty much like life in a Western country. Kids go to school and come home to do homework, play video games, watch TV, and hit the sack. Life in the smaller villages is more traditional and might include chopping wood, tending animals, doing dishes and laundry by hand, and drawing water from a well.

Getting Around

Romanians may be very polite, but their driving style is aggressive! Those who own cars tend to drive fast in the city, on the highway, or up a mountain road. Bigger city streets are really crowded, and traffic jams are frequent. (The capital of Bucharest alone has more than 1 million cars). The driving is made more difficult by the need to stop suddenly for stray animals, potholes, or horse carts. (You'll even see horse carts on modern intercity two-lane highways.) Watch your speed if you decide to drive in Romania. The police have modern radar equipment, and the traffic fines are stiff!

Getting places in big cities is much easier by taxi, metro (subway), or bus. Getting to other cities in the country is easier by bus or train. The buses are small, crowded, and frequently don't run on time. The train system is a better bet.

Romania's railway network is the fourth largest in Europe. Trains service every town, city, and even many remote villages. It's easy to get tickets. Different types of trains suit different travel needs. Personal trains stop at every station on their route. Semi-slow trains stop in towns but not villages. Rapid trains cover many miles in between each stop, so they're good for traveling long distances. Intercity trains are ideal for business travelers because they offer air conditioning, reading lights, power plugs, and Wi-Fi. Much of the railroad system throughout Romania is being upgraded as part of the government's infrastructure project.

Shop 'Til You Drop!

Got the urge to shop? There are plenty of places to do it in Romania – old and new, small and large, and indoors and outdoors.

Farmer's Markets

Farmers' markets offer the freshest Romanian produce straight from the fields. Much of the food is organic—that is, it is produced without fertilizers or additives, and it's probably just been picked. Savor the crunch of fresh sunflower seeds or a juicy berry or two. Don't forget to haggle. It's expected for the farmer to offer one price, the buyer to counter with another, and both to reach an agreement. Haggling is half the fun of going to the market!

Hypermarkets

No haggling here! You'll find lots of stuff, especially in the Bucharest hypermarkets. They're big, new, sparkling, and filled with quality goods from Romania and the rest of Europe. The items may be more expensive than those found elsewhere in the country, but you're guaranteed to have a hassle-free shopping experience. You'll find everything from food and beverages to clothing.

'Alimentară'

These are old food stores of the Communist era. They're less expensive and definitely less attractive than hypermarkets. You'll usually find them in the smaller towns. They sell quality food and other items, but you might not be able to pluck them from the shelf yourself. One clerk may give you the items you want, another may total your order, and another may take your money. The benefit of these stores is their personal service. The people who run 'alimentar ' are a valuable part of the neighborhood.

Country Fairs

Here's where you'll get a great glimpse of old Romania. The traditional weekly country fair is usually held on a Sunday. It's as much a social event as a shopping experience. Amid dancing, amusement rides, and food stalls, you can buy animals, clothing, locally produced foods and crafts – even used cars and tractors! Lots of haggling goes on and lots of people attend. Some fairs draw thousands of people from neighboring villages. Spending a few hours at the fair is a great way to catch up with friends and relatives.

Going to School

The Romanian educational system has been continually reformed since the Romanian Revolution of 1989. Kids between ages three and six can go to kindergarten, but this isn't required. They must start school at age seven, however, and stay in school until age 16 or 17 (Grade 10). There is also a private tutoring system available. Most kids use it during secondary school to prepare for the extremely difficult exams that will help them pursue further education.

Famous Romanians

People all over the globe still talk about the famous Romanian gymnast Nadia Comăneci (ko-man-ech) (1961–). At the 1976 Summer Olympic Games, she became the first gymnast ever to score a perfect ten. By age fifteen, she had won three gold medals, one silver medal, and one bronze. In the 1980 Summer Olympics, she won two gold and two silver medals. Today, she lives in Oklahoma, where she works with many charities.

Johnny Weissmuller (1904–1984), who is best known for playing Tarzan in the movies, was born in Romania. One of the world's best swimmers in the 1920s, he won six Olympic medals and 52 U.S. National Championships. He set 67 world swimming records. He's still best known for his role as Tarzan—and for that famous Tarzan yell!

Movie tough guy Edward Goldenberg Robinson, Sr. (1893–1973) was one of the most famous actors of his time, playing lots of gangsters and many other parts. Even today, he's still one of film's most famous faces.

Nicolae Paulescu (1869–1931) was a Romanian medical professor who discovered insulin. Used to treat diabetes, insulin is one of the world's greatest medical breakthroughs.

Did You Know?

The Palace of Parliament in the Romanian capital of Bucharest is the second largest office building in the world, after the U.S. Pentagon in Arlington, Virginia.

Transylvania means *land beyond the forest*.

The film *Cold Mountain*, starring Jude Law, Nicole Kidman, and Renee Zellweger, was filmed on location in Romania.

Ten cities in the United States have sister cities in Romania! Bucharest is the sister city of Atlanta, Georgia. Brasov is the sister city of Cleveland, Ohio.

You probably already know of the famous novel *Twenty Thousand Leagues under the Sea* by science fiction writer Jules Verne. He also wrote a novel inspired by Romania's castles called *The Carpathian Castle*.

Count Dracula, the fictional character created by Irish writer Bram Stoker, was inspired by Vlad Dracula. He ruled Walachia at various times from 1456 to 1462. Although his methods were extremely cruel, some Romanians still call him a hero for repelling invaders. As for Stoker, he never actually visited Romania. His 1897 novel *Dracula* was not published in Romanian until 1990.

Language & Expressions

Here are some fun facts about verbal and nonverbal communication in Romania.

Famous Romanian Proverbs

Here are ten famous Romanian proverbs. What do you think they mean?

A creaking door hangs longest.
Abundance, like want, ruins many.
Do not cut the bough you are sitting on.
Do not rake up old grievances.
Fortune is made of glass.
Long absent, soon forgotten.
Under a ragged coat lies wisdom.
What the heart thinks, the tongue speaks.
A small leak sinks a great ship.
Streams go, rocks remain.

Body Language and Etiquette in Romania

Here are some examples of body language and etiquette you'll find in Romania.

You may be requested to take off your shoes before you enter a home or apartment.

Address a person by title (Mr., Miss, Ms., Mrs., Dr.) and last name until the person invites you to use his or her first name.

Many Romanians think that moving air isn't healthy. So even if a room is hot, they won't open doors and windows to get the air moving.

Romanians are very hospitable to tourists.

If dining in a Romanian home, the host will insist on visitors taking just one more helping—even if they refuse. Romanians think it's polite for visitors to refuse and polite for them to insist.

Romanians dine with their napkins on the table and not in their lap. They also dine with their hands visible, wrists on the table.

Friends and family kiss each other on both cheeks when they greet and leave each other. Some older Romanians might kiss a woman's hand when greeting her.

If you are invited to a Romanian home, bring candy or flowers as a gift. You should bring an odd number of flowers. Even numbers of flowers are given for funerals.

Respect toward elders is expected. Older people are seen as wise.

If visiting a church or a monastery, your clothing should cover your shoulders and knees. Ideally, women should wear skirts, and men should wear trousers. Orthodox women cover their hair in church.

If you are visiting Romania, know the history and avoid discussions about politics or about the various ethnic groups that live in the country. Some ethnic groups still don't get along with each other.

Know before You Go

Here are some common phrases you will use in Romania. The spelling and pronunciation are also given. Try them out! Look up some additional ones!

English	Romanian	Pronunciation
Good day.	Bună Ziua.	boo-nuh zee-wah
Good morning.	Bună dimineața.	boo-nuh dee-mee-nyah-tsah
Good evening.	Bună seara.	boo-nuh syah-rah
Good night. (at bed-time)	Noapte bună.	nwahp-teh boo-nuh
Yes	Da	dah
No	Nu	noo
Nice to meet you.	Îmi pare bine.	um pah-reh bee-neh
I'm sorry.	Îmi pare rău.	um pah-reh row
Thank you.	Mulțumesc.	mool-tsoo-mesk
You're welcome	Cu plăcere.	coo pluh-cheh-reh
1	unu	oo-noo
2	doi	doy
3	trei	tray
4	patru	pah-troo
5	cinci	cheench
6	șase	shah-seh
7	șapte	shahp-teh
8	opt	opt
9	nouă	noh-uh
10	zece	zeh-cheh

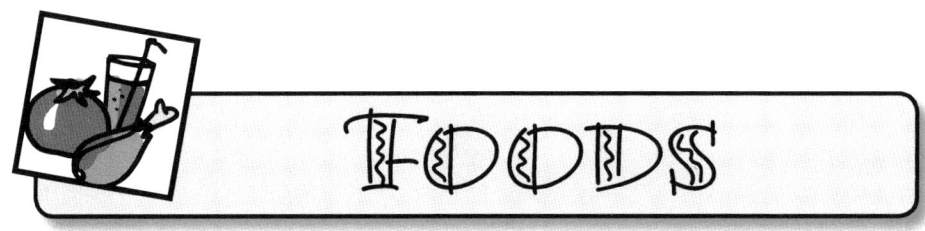

Foods

Romania's long history of being occupied by Romans, Turks, Hungarians, Germans, Poles, and Russians makes the country's food a unique blend of cuisines. The flavor comes from the way foods are prepared. While Romania has its share of microwaves, people still cook in clay roasting pans and iron kettles—especially in the country. Using centuries-old recipes, methods, and cookware gives the food a home-cooked taste.

Common Local Dishes

Most Romanian restaurants serve Romanian food only, so it helps to know a bit about the dishes, the seasonings, and what to expect.

Polenta

Mamaliga is the Romanian version of polenta (a thick cornmeal mush boiled in water). *Bulz* is roasted polenta filled with cheese, bacon, and sour cream.

Polenta

Meat and Fish

Pork is the most popular meat in Romania, but beef, lamb, and fish are part of the national menu, too. Meat dishes include *friptura* (steak) and *salata boef* (a salad of chopped, cooked vegetables and meat topped with mayonnaise, tomatoes, and parsley). *Tochitura* is fried meat and sausages served in a special sauce with polenta and fried eggs. *Mici* is spicy sausage cooked on the barbeque. *Drob* is a casserole made from lamb or pork liver and kidneys. The Romanian version of a hamburger is a slice of ham on a burger bun, topped with a slice of cheese and a layer of French fries! Other local dishes you might need to develop a taste for are cow tongue, chicken liver, and pork liver.

Common fish dishes include fish eggs (caviar), vegetable and fish stew, fish cakes, fish in a creamy paprika sauce, fish in salty brine, and breaded fish.

Soups, Sides, and Salads

Many of the meat and vegetable soups are soured with ingredients such as lemon juice, vinegar, or sauerkraut juice. Common soups are white tripe (sheep or goat stomach) soup, calf foot soup, fish soup, and a red vegetable soup called *ciorba* (chor-ba) *taraneasca*.

Pickled green tomatoes and pickled watermelon are popular side dishes.

You'll find garlic and onions both on the table and cooked into the food. People eat garlic and onions raw and in special sauces. *Mujdei* (mooj-dā) is a traditional sauce made of garlic, olive oil, and spices. Onion salad is just that—diced onions! Bulgarian salads are a mix of onions, lettuce, tomatoes, cheese, white sauce, and ham.

Bread

Bread comes with every meal, but you might not get butter. Instead, people flavor their bread with herbs and other ingredients, such as dill.

Cheese

Even in the 21st century, Romanian farmers still do not use chemicals or additives in their soil. Their sheep, cows, and goats are fed on fresh grass and clean spring water. Thus, the milk these animals produce is made into some of the freshest, most delicious cheese in the world. If you stay at a country farm (many farmers provide bed and breakfast for tourists), you'll be treated to fine cheese at every meal. This includes hard cheese, soft cheese, cheese for toasting on bread, cheese for crumbling on salads, and much more!

Desserts

Romanians don't wait for a big meal to eat dessert. Even the smallest daily meal might end with a considerable treat. Traditional desserts include *pandispan* (this means *Spanish bread*, a cake filled with sour cherries). Also popular are all sorts of cakes, puddings, custards, doughnuts, pretzels, stuffed pancakes, and baklava (thin pastry filled with nuts and sweetened with honey).

Special Holiday Foods

Easter and Christmas are the most important Orthodox holidays of the year. They're also eagerly awaited days of feasting on traditional foods.

Turkish Delight

Christmas

On December 20, St. Ignatius's day, each family in the country slaughters a pig and uses it to create many traditional foods, including: ham; spicy sausage; sausage made with liver; pan-fried pork; and dishes made of the pig's feet, head, and ears in a spicy jelly called aspic.

Dessert will include *cozonac* (cake bread served at Christmas or Easter) and Turkish Delight (jelly-like cubes coated with icing and dusted with sugar).

Easter

An Easter dinner of roast lamb is the most traditional meal of the year. Romanian lamb haggis is another traditional favorite. It's made of minced heart, liver, and lungs from a sheep or calf, which has been mixed with seasoning and roasted. Sheep brains are also considered an Easter delicacy.

Along with *cozonac*, the traditional Easter cake is *pască*—a pie made of yeast dough with a sweet cottage cheese or chocolate filling.

Fast Food, Snacks, and Street Food

Pizza Hut®, McDonald's®, KFC®, and other familiar fast food restaurants are easily found in the bigger Romanian cities. However, the fast food is not that much cheaper than the food you can find in other restaurants.

Street food vendors and small food shops abound, especially in the urban areas. It's easy to grab a snack on the run, whether you're looking for a quick meal or a tasty treat. For a very reasonable price, you can get hot pretzels, *langoşi* (hot cheese-filled dough), donuts and pastries, *mici* (spicy meat patties), and meat kebabs. Thin pancakes filled with chocolate and jam or bananas and ice cream are popular, too.

Holidays & Festivals

The Christmas Season

The Romanian Christmas season starts six weeks before Christmas when people begin a fast. This means they eat no animal products like meat, eggs, fish, milk, or cheese.

St. Nicholas Day (December 6)

On this day, children polish their shoes and leave them in front of a window. The tradition is that St. Nicholas fills their shoes with small gifts.

The Week before Christmas

Decorating the tree, singing carols, and eating traditional foods are all part of the exciting days leading up to Christmas. Three days before Christmas, walnut and raisin cakes are baked. Two days before Christmas the cooking for the Christmas feast begins.

Christmas Eve (December 24)

This day is reserved for decorating the Christmas tree, followed by a large family dinner. After dark, the kids go caroling door to door, and the adults stay home to greet them with candy, fruit, baked goods, and even money. Romanian kids believe that Santa leaves presents under the tree for the entire family when they are asleep.

Christmas (December 25 and 26)

Christmas Day is celebrated with friends, family, and feasting. Groups of adults go caroling at night. When they finish, they'll be invited into each house for food, a hot drink, and maybe even a gift!

December 26 is an official holiday, giving everyone a rest and time to prepare for the New Year.

New Year's Eve (December 31)

This is one holiday the whole country celebrates well into the night. It's commonly believed that no one should spend the night alone. So friends get together to wish each other a happy life and prosperity for the coming year. Children are usually given apples, nuts, and home-baked breads.

New Year's Day (January 1)

New Year's Day is celebrated with songs about health and happiness, dance, and lots of food! Sometimes the performers even wear masks and costumes. Wheat appears as the traditional symbol of wealth and prosperity. Kids may start the day wishing everyone a Happy New Year by touching them with a special bouquet of twigs and colored paper flowers called the *Sorcova*. They'll get all kinds of treats in return, like money, candy, pretzels, and cookies.

January 6

This day is commonly thought to be the coldest of the year. It celebrates the christening of Christ.

The Easter Season • *March, April, or early May*

Easter is Romania's second most important religious celebration. The official holiday includes not only Easter itself but the day after, Easter Monday.

People generally observe a six-week fast before the holiday, eating no meat or animal products. They spend the time preparing traditional foods for Easter dinner like special pastries and cheese.

On Flowers Sunday, the Sunday before Easter, all who have names associated with flowers (Rose and Lily, for example) have a special celebration. Fish may be eaten on this day.

The ritual of coloring eggs is very traditional in Romania. Certain customs are always observed to honor the symbolism of the egg as a miracle of creation. The first egg colored is for the children. It must be red and placed in the children's room to protect them from harm. The second egg, colored blue, is meant to bring good luck in a marriage.

On Easter Eve, people eat no food. Before going to the church, they wash their faces in a bowl of water that also contains red Easter eggs and a silver coin. They do this in the belief that they will be as healthy as the eggs and will have more money! They may even take a bowl of Easter eggs to be blessed at the beautiful midnight church service that will include a candle procession. They try to keep the candles lit until they come home after the service for the first of several Easter meals.

On Easter morning it is customary for family members to knock eggs! The person who has the egg that doesn't crack is said to be the luckier person.

Martisor (Mar-tsē-shor) • *March 1*

This holiday signifies the end of cold winter and the arrival of sunny spring. Girls and women are given a small and thoughtful gift (a martisor), such as a plant, shells, flowers, or even animals—along with red and white ribbons that symbolize life and purity. The gifts are said to bring good luck throughout the month of March and the coming year.

Labor Day • *May 1*

Similar to Labor Day, this holiday celebrates the achievements of workers. Celebrations include parades and patriotic events, but, people mostly celebrate by getting together for some great food and conversation.

Saint Mary's Day • *August 15*

This religious holiday celebrates the Assumption of Mary, the mother of Christ, into Heaven. It is also designated as a special day for the Romanian Navy, of which St. Mary is the patron saint.

National Day • *December 1*

This treasured national holiday celebrates the Great Union of Transylvania with Romania in December of 1918. It became an official national holiday after the Romanian Revolution of 1989. It also marks the unification of the provinces of Banat, Bessarabia, and Bukovina with Romania.

Saint's Name Days

All over Romania, people celebrate their saint's name day, which is considered even more important than a birthday. People traditionally attend a church service on their name day. They may start the day with a hymn to the saint included in the family's morning prayers. They will display a picture of the saint or take it to church. People may even have an open house for family and friends with all the festivity of a birthday party.

Festivals and Other Special Events

Festivals filled with fun, food, music, and dance fill the Romanian calendar just about every month of the year. With each yearly festival, Romanians preserve their traditions and hand them down to the next generation. They celebrate life events, the arts, folklore, and traditional country life. Here are just three of the events held every summer.

Traditional Crafts Fair (June): Folk art is very much alive in Romania! At this special event, master craftsmen from all over the country meet at the Village Museum in Bucharest to give demonstrations in traditional folk art, such as woodcarving, weaving, embroidering, and egg painting. Thousands flock to this fair every year.

Bucharest of Old (July): The city celebrates the way it was 150 years ago. The capital is packed with people who come for the parade of 1800s costumes and horse-drawn carriages. Food, music, and special performances round out the fun.

Dance at Prislop (August): This festival celebrates the ties among Transylvania, Moldova, and Maramures, Romania's three main regions. Villagers parade in folk costume to Prislop Pass in the Carpathian Mountains and then celebrate with traditional dancing, music, and lots of great food.

Creative Arts

The folk artists of Romania are famous throughout the world for their handcrafted masterpieces. Despite the many years of upheaval in the country, much Romanian folk art has survived the centuries. Woodworking, weaving, egg painting, and other folk arts are thriving today, thanks to the many artisans all over the country keeping their crafts alive and sharing them with others.

Fabric Arts

Weaving by hand using homespun wool, cotton, raw silk, and flax is a flourishing folk art. Each region of Romania has its own designs and produces its own type of hand-woven items. Transylvania, for example, produces rugs. It's common for people to decorate their houses with hand-woven fabrics and pass them down over the generations.

Wood Carvings

Like hand-woven fabric, hand-carved Romanian creations are not just for tourists. They're treasured by Romanian city folks and country folks alike. Household items like spoons, chests, benches, cupboards, and musical instruments have honored places in many homes. The designs are intricate and traditional. The wood comes straight from the Romanian forests.

Pottery

No one is quite sure which civilization to thank for Romanian pottery—the Romans, the Dacians, or another of the country's many inhabitants over the centuries. Today, there are more than 200 pottery centers all over the country, each with its own unique designs.

Hand Painting

Hand painting is an ancient craft. The Romanians have taken it to great heights with their paintings on glass and wood. Often showing religious themes, saints, or scenes from daily life, Romanian painting is known for its bright colors and stylized characters that look a little other-worldly! This craft still thrives, especially in Transylvania. Beautiful collections of painted glass are found in the Romanian Art Museum in Bucharest and in the famous Brukenthal Museum in the city of Sibiu.

And then there are those famous Romanian Easter eggs! Who would have thought that an egg could become a treasured art object? Romanian painted eggs are simply spectacular. The intricate, traditional designs painted on hollowed out eggshells are one of the world's best-loved folk arts. Particularly in rural areas, folk artists spend the weeks before Easter preparing these delicate creations. They empty the eggs, paint them with fine pencils in complicated patterns, and coat them with a solution that makes them hard and preserves the artwork.

Architecture

Wooden Homes and Churches

Travel through the countryside, and you'll see wooden homes decorated with elaborate carvings. Travel through Maramureş in northern Transylvania, and you'll see wooden churches so striking and unusual that they are listed on the UNESCO list of World Heritage Sites. These famous churches, built during the 17th and 18th centuries, were essentially a solution to a problem. At the time, it was forbidden to build stone churches. So craftsmen built these tall-spired churches *without* nails! They generally have tall towers above the entrance, a steep roof, and a tall bell tower. They're dark inside, which adds to their mysterious beauty.

Painted Monasteries

In Northern Moldavia, a group of monasteries from the 15th and 16th centuries have spectacular exterior mural paintings. The frescoes feature saints, prophets, Jesus, and images of the afterlife. The paintings were designed to tell the story of the Bible and the lives of the saints to the local villages. Like Romania's wooden churches, these monasteries are constructed of timber and fashioned in the Gothic architectural style. Several of these monasteries, are on the UNESCO World Heritage Site list.

Castles and Fortresses

There are so many castles and fortresses across Romania that you might think it really is a land of fairy tales. Castles and fortresses built from the 14th to the 18th century were used to defend the country. They're fairly plain and stark. Those built in the late 1800s and after, however, are luxurious—and huge! Many are popular tourist spots that are well maintained, surrounded by countryside, and filled with priceless art. The most famous is Transylvania's Bran Castle, built in the 1300s. This was supposed to be the home of the legendary Dracula. Although it really wasn't, tourists flock to it anyway. It's now a museum with a large collection of furniture, weapons, armor, and a considerable amount of mystery!

Bran Castle

Traditional Music, Dance, and Costumes

The many festivals in the country assure that Romanian folk music and folk dance remain alive and well. The true heart of Romania comes out in its music and dance. The music is easily recognizable, thanks to the *cetera* (a high-toned violin), the *zongora* (a larger violin), and the *doba* (a goatskin and wood drum).

The dances, whether done in groups or with partners, are fast and lively, often with hand clapping and singing. The dancers wear the folk costume distinctive to their region. Both the men's and women's costumes usually have white clothing with colorfully embroidered, wide-sleeved shirts. The women wear bright aprons and head scarves. The men wear wide belts, embroidered sheepskin vests, boots, and hats.

Sports & Games

Sports

Romanians love sports. The government supports sports programs; many kids who show athletic talent will likely get special training to develop their skills. You may not think of Romania when you think of Olympic champions—but think again! Romania ranks 15th overall in medals at the Summer Olympic Games. Of the 283 medals it has won over the years, 82 of them are gold.

Gymnastics

Romanians *really* show their stuff to the world in gymnastics, especially where the ladies are concerned. In 1976, the whole world came to know Romania through the Summer Olympic Games, when Nadia Comăneci became the first gymnast to score a perfect 10 at the Olympics. She ended her Olympic career with nine scores of 10, as well as nine medals (five in 1976, four in 1980; five of these were gold medals).

Lots of Romanian kids who have athletic talent—both girls and boys—study this ancient sport from the time they are young. Not all of them will make it to the Olympics. But they'll take it seriously and spend hours training in a fine athletic facility or special school and competing at various skill levels.

Football

Football (soccer) is Romania's most popular sport. You'll see kids all over Romania kicking around the football during breaks and after school. They'll more than likely watch lots of football on TV, too. Romania has several national football teams, and the people are avid football fans! The Romanian National Football Team, which is the best known team in the country, has played in the Football World Cup seven times. It reached the quarterfinals in the 1994 World Cup held in the United States.

Handball

Team Handball is extremely popular. Two teams pass and bounce a ball with the object of throwing it into the opposing team's goal. The team with the most goals after two 30-minute periods wins. Romanian kids love this game, and it's a popular professional sport, too. The Romanian men's national handball team has won the Handball World Cup four times since 1961. Since 1972, it has won four Olympic medals. The Romanian women's team won the Handball World Cup in 1962.

Other Sports

Romanian kids love basketball almost as much as they love soccer! Gheorghe Mureșan was the first Romanian to enter the National Basketball Association (NBA). At 7' 7", he was the tallest man ever to play in the NBA. His professional career ended in 2000, after playing for the Washington Bullets and New Jersey Nets.

Oina is a traditional Romanian sport similar to baseball, but the game is much shorter and each team has eleven players instead of nine. *Oina* was originally played by Romanian shepherds. There are two *Oina* Federations in Romania.

Games

Chess is the most popular table game in Romania. It's common to see retired folks playing chess in the park on warm days. Romania even has a Chess Federation. Since 1946, the Romanian Chess Championship has been held yearly, with national contests determining both men's and women's final teams.

MP5126 – Romania

"FAZAN" (CHAINED WORDS)

Number of Players Needed
5 to 10

Directions
1. The first player begins the game by speaking or writing one word in which the last two letters can begin another word.
   Example: FIRST.

2. The second player must think of a word beginning with the last two letters of the first player's word.
   Example: ST = STORE.

3. The second player then gives a word to the third player.
   Example: TOOTH.

4. The third player must find a word beginning with the last two letters of the second player's word.
   Example: TH = THEIR.

5. Play continues. A person who cannot come up with a word is out of the game!

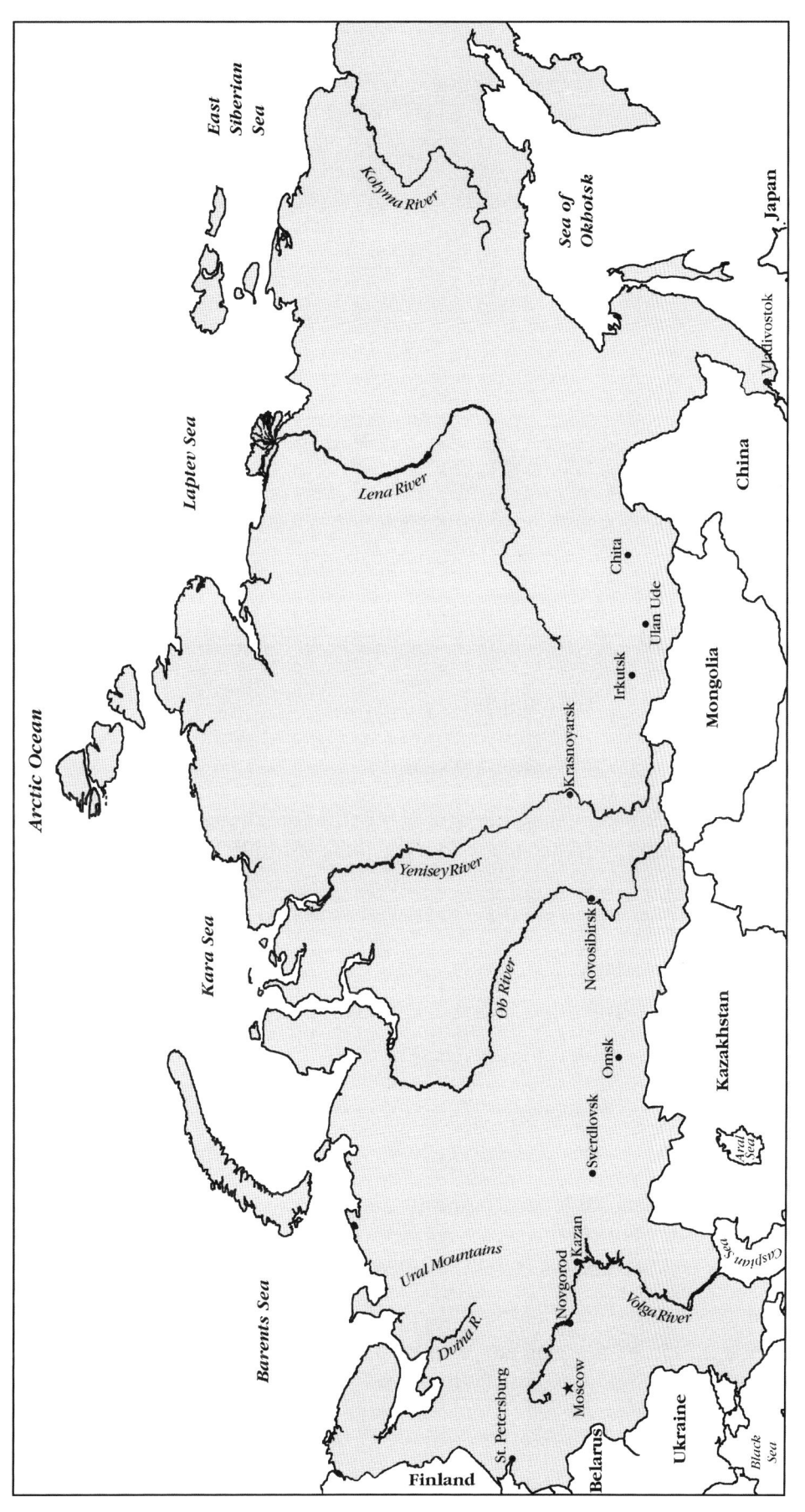

MP5126 – Russia

WELCOME TO RUSSIA!

Moving into the modern world, but still mysterious, Russia is the largest country on Earth. Between 1917 and 1991, the Russian Republic was the center of the Soviet Union, which was a world superpower. Russia has now returned to its prerevolutionary status as an independent country. It still has great influence in the Commonwealth of Independent States (which replaced the Soviet Union) and in the United Nations.

Russia has had one of the darkest and most brutal histories of any country in the world. Although the political situation is getting better, we still know relatively little about what really goes on there. Nevertheless, this vast land is endlessly fascinating. Its spectacular scenery, unique architecture, incredible culture, and rich resources make it one of the top places on the globe that people want to know more about.

FAST FACTS

Official Name: Russian Federation

Location: Northern Asia, bordering the Arctic Ocean, between Europe and the North Pacific Ocean

Population: 140,041,247 (2010 estimate)

Capital City: Moscow

Area: 6,592,800 square miles. Russia is about 1.8 times the size of the United States. It is the largest country in the world in terms of area.

Major Language: Russian

Major Religion: Russian Orthodox: 15–20%
Muslim: 10–15%
Russia has large numbers of nonpracticing Christians and atheists due to the former Soviet rule that forbade religious practice.

Currency: The ruble (bank notes and coins)   1 ruble = 100 kopecks
There are 1, 5, 10, 15, 20, and 50 kopeck pieces.

Climate: Most of Russia has long, cold winters and mild to warm, short summers. In northeastern Siberia, January temperatures average below –50 °F. Rainfall is moderate in most of Russia. Snow covers more than half of the country six months each year.

The Land: Russia covers a large part of Europe and Asia. It has coastlines on the Arctic Ocean, Baltic Sea, Black Sea, Caspian Sea, and Pacific Ocean. It borders eight European countries, three Asian countries, and three countries with land in both Europe and Asia. Much of the west is a large plain with low hills. The Ural Mountains separate Europe and Asia. Siberia, which is east of the Urals, has low western plains, a central plateau, and an eastern mountainous wilderness.

Type of Government:	Russia is a federation and a semi-presidential republic. The President is the head of state. The Prime Minister is the head of government.
Flag:	The Russian flag, which has been official since 2000, is three equal horizontal bands of white (at the top), blue, and red. The government has not given any particular meaning to the colors.
Coat of Arms:	Adopted in 1993, Russia's Coat of Arms contains the Russian state symbols—the two-headed eagle with its wings spread upward and the mounted figure slaying a serpent or dragon—and the three imperial crowns of Russia joined by a ribbon. The images are set on a red heraldic shield. The eagle holds an orb and scepter in its talons, which are traditional signs of a monarch's power—even though Russia is a federation and not a monarchy.
National Flower:	Chamomile (Matricaria Recutita). This flower is in the daisy family.
National Tree:	White birch
Motto:	"God is with Us"

Natural Environment

Russia occupies major parts of Europe and Asia. It is about 4,000 miles wide and includes eleven time zones! Flying east from Moscow to Vladivostok takes longer than flying from Moscow to New York.

The vast eastern region of Russia is called Siberia. Think of Siberia and the popular images of a frozen wasteland where criminals are sent for punishment probably come to mind. This is only partly true. Like the rest of the country, Siberia is a combination of geographical regions that is not totally cold and deserted. Much of Russia's great mineral wealth of coal, oil, gas, uranium, and gold is found there. Many long rivers in Siberia—the Ob, the Yenisey, (yen-i-sāy) the Lena, and the Kolyma (ka-lee-ma) —are major transportation routes, as well as sources of water and irrigation for crops.

The major types of geography found in Russia are the tundra, the forests, and the steppes. The tundra is the northernmost land around the Arctic Circle. This land is frozen most of the year and only thaws on the surface during the short, hot summer. The frozen ground is called permafrost. The land underneath is rich with gas and minerals.

The people of the tundra include nomadic tribes called the Yakuts, Chukchis, and Nentsy. They are similar in appearance and lifestyle to the American Inuit. They have always made their living by herding reindeer, which they use for many necessities. The Soviet government tried to formally organize these tribes, but had only limited success. In recent years, the people of northern Siberia have become concerned about the destruction of their environment by hunters and by natural gas and mining operations.

South of the tundra lies a great forest region filled with pine, spruce, birch, and other trees. Early Slavic people began their settlement in the western part of these forest lands, along the great rivers called the Dnieper (nee-per), Oka, Dvina, and Volga. They cleared the forests for farms and built their houses and churches of wood. They became skilled woodcarvers, and modern Russian craftspeople still follow some of their ways. The ancient cities of Kiev and Novgorod began in the great forests south of the tundra.

MP5126 – Russia

The open grasslands south of the forests are called steppes. They extend all the way from the western border of the Ukraine to the southwestern part of Siberia. The steppes contain some of the best farmland in Russia and the Ukraine (a country in Eastern Europe, bordered by Russia on the east).

Russia has several major mountain ranges. The Ural Mountains run 1,500 miles north to south and divide Europe and Asia. The entire southern area between Russia, Mongolia, and China is a combination of various mountain ranges.

Ural Mountains

Plants and Animals

In the tundra, you'll primarily find mosses, lichens (a fungus that grows on tree trunks and rocks), sedges (grass-like plants), and shrubs. Wheat is grown in western Siberia. Along the coast are the polar bear, walrus, and seal. Inland are reindeer and other furry creatures like the arctic fox, sable, hare, and ermine. There are many waterfowl here, too, like ducks and geese.

The forests south of the tundra are the most extensive in the world. The taiga, a coniferous forest that includes pine trees (called the *yolka*) and fir trees, makes up the northern and central part of the forest belt. (The *yolka* is the traditional holiday tree decorated at New Year's.) The southern forest belt is made up of deciduous trees like oak, elm, maple, and miles upon miles of birch. The forests are teeming with wildlife, such as brown bears, wolves, elk, deer, lynxes, foxes, sables, badgers, and more than 200 species of birds.

The steppe is similar to the North American prairies. The northern forest steppe is made up of grasslands and deciduous forests. Some of Russia's richest soil is found here. The open steppe below the northern forest is made up almost entirely of grassland. There are few large animals here, except for antelope and the wolf. However, you'll find small burrowing animals like ground squirrels, lemmings, moles, rabbits, rats, and skunks. There are also many kinds of birds, like hawks.

A History of Russia

Settlement by Early Tribes

Today's Russians descended from various tribes that settled in the western forest regions between the Baltic and Black Seas. The Scythians ruled the area from 700 to 200 BCE. The Sarmatians followed, ruling from 200 BCE to 200 CE. Both groups traded widely with other civilized cultures, like the Greeks. Scythian gold work was a highly prized trade item.

After 200 CE, other tribes, such as the Goths, Huns, Avars, and Rhazars, invaded this area and mixed with the tribes already there. In the 800s, a seafaring people from northern Europe came down to the Dvina and Dnieper rivers to trade. The natives called them *Rus*. This is how Russia got its name. Rurik, the leader of the Rus, became a protector and later a ruler of the region.

Capitals of Early Russia

The capital of the early Russian nation was Kiev, until feuds between various princes caused divisions. In 1237, Mongols from the Far East invaded Russia and ruled for about 250 years. During this time, the princes of Russia tolerated and even paid tribute to the Mongols. However, in about 1480, the princes of Moscow and the surrounding towns drove out the Mongols and established their own rule. From then until the time of Peter the Great, the city of Moscow was the center and capital of the country.

In 1703, Tsar (zar) (which means *emperor* or *ruler*) Peter, who ruled Russia from 1682 to 1725, moved the capital to a new city he had built on the Finnish Gulf. Called St. Petersburg, the city was a much-needed northern seaport and a window to the West. Peter wanted Russia to learn the ways of Western Europe. St. Petersburg, later renamed Leningrad (after the 20th century revolutionary Vladimir Lenin), became a showplace for the arts and architecture. Today, the city is again called St. Petersburg.

Russian Leaders

Russia has had many leaders and heroes. Here are some of the most important people who helped shape its long history.

Vladimir, Prince of Kiev, adopted Christianity as the official religion of the country in 988.

Saint Alexander Nevsky (nev-skee), Prince of Novgorod, defeated the Swedes, the Germans, and the Lithuanians when each group tried to invade Russia. Nevsky is one of the key figures of medieval Russia. He lived from 1220 to 1263.

Ivan the Great (Ivan III) expanded Russia by conquering lands in the east, west, and south. He took the title of Tsar of All the Russian Land. He lived from 1462 to 1505 and was one of the longest-reigning Russian rulers. The two-headed eagle on the Russian Coat of Arms was adopted during his reign.

Ivan the IV (called Ivan the Terrible) was the grandson of Ivan the Great. A leader who was greatly feared, he conquered many of Russia's enemies. However, he tortured and killed many of his own people as well, including his own son. He lived from 1533 to 1584.

Empress Catherine II (called Catherine the Great) carried on the work of modernizing and promoting education and the arts. In fact, no Russian leader before or after her did as much to help develop the arts in Russia. Under her rule, Russia became a great power of Europe and added about 200,000 miles to its territory. She lived from 1762 to 1796.

Tsar Alexander II ruled Russia from 1855 until his assassination in 1881. In 1861, he freed the Russian serfs from their bondage to their masters.

The Russian Revolution

By 1917, Russia was in serious decline. Fighting against the Germans in World War I had proved to be a disaster. The German army was better trained, better equipped, and had more food. By the end of October 1916, Russia had lost nearly 5 million men.

As a result of the war, Russia experienced widespread food shortages and very high prices. Few could afford what little food was available. The economy was beginning to crumble. The government was weak and corrupt. People were in great despair.

Those employed in the crowded major cities developed a working class that was being exposed to Western ideas about workers' rights. People wanted more democratic participation in government instead of a monarch who was the country's ultimate ruler. Workers went on strike to protest their poverty and bad working conditions. The protests and strikes often resulted in violence and death.

Nicholas II, the last tsar of Russia, was blamed for all of these crises—particularly the bad economy and the loss in World War I. He ignored the people's demands for a constitutional government. Under what is now called the February Revolution of 1917, his regime collapsed. He and his family were executed a year later.

In October of that year, Vladimir Lenin led the Bolshevik Revolution of 1917 (a key event in the Russian Revolution), and destroyed the Russian monarchy. This led to the creation of the Soviet Union in 1922 with Lenin as its leader. It marks the beginning of modern Soviet history. It also introduced the world to Communism.

Communism is a political philosophy *and* a form of government. The main idea behind Communism is that society has only one working class (instead of the rich, the middle-class, and the poor). People in this class share in the ownership of property and together decide what will be produced and what policies will be made. Under Communism, there is only one political party: the Community Party. It is loyal to the teachings and leadership of Lenin and Karl Marx (a German author whose writings on Communism influenced Bolshevik leaders such as Lenin).

Lenin became the hero of the people during the era of Communist rule. Little children were taught to love and respect him.

Vladimir Lenin

Joseph Stalin, Lenin's successor, was respected but feared for his brutality. He became a dictator, and millions died as a result of his harsh policies. He helped transform Russia from a farming society into a highly industrialized nation. In later years, Stalin was denounced by some Russian leaders, including Nikita Khrushchev (kru-shev), who was Premier of the Soviet Union from 1958 to 1964.

The Breakup of the Soviet Union

Mikhail Gorbachev (mi-kī-el gor-ba-chof) came to leadership in the Soviet Union in 1985. He allowed many changes to occur in an attempt to modernize the country. This eventually led to the overthrow of the Community Party and the breakup of the Soviet Union. During the last years of the Soviet Union, the economy was again in near-collapse, as it had been in Tsar Nicholas' last years. There were severe food shortages and very high prices. In 1992, there was an unsuccessful military coup against Gorbachev. The coup was led by Communist party members who felt Gorbachev had gone too far in his reform efforts. Instead of preserving the Soviet Union, however, the coup resulted in its collapse. In 1990, Gorbachev was awarded the Nobel Peace Prize.

A New Russia Emerges

The Soviet Union was officially dissolved in 1991. That same year, Boris Yeltsin was elected the first President of Russia in the first direct presidential election in Russian history. Yeltsin had the difficult job of leading the country to democracy and creating a market economy based on supply and demand. This transition was very hard for Russia, and it continues to be difficult. State-owned businesses became privatized (that is, they are now owned by private individuals). Much of the country's wealth fell into the hands of very few people. Many others fell into poverty.

After many years of the country's internal struggle, Yeltsin resigned. He handed his position to Prime Minister Vladimir Putin, who was elected Russia's second President in 2000. The Russian economy grew under Putin, but many people (particularly in the West) have criticized his actions, such as restricting freedom of the press. Nevertheless, his approval rating in Russia remains high. In 2008, Dmitry (du-mee-tree) Medvedev was elected President of Russia. Putin became the country's Prime Minister.

Russia Today

Russia was once called the "sleeping bear." Now the bear is slowly waking up! Formerly closed-off areas of Russia are being opened for tourism. Reconstruction is taking place in many parts of the country, particularly in the major cities. Architecture is being restored. The arts are flourishing again. Russian athletes continue to be top international competitors. And although many Russians are still struggling economically, they are beginning to feel that the country is moving out of its isolation to take its place as a vital part of the greater world.

Daily Life

Russians are deeply proud of their country. Daily life is not easy, but they pride themselves on being able to overcome hardships and enjoy life. Patriotic poems and songs are an essential part of the culture. Russians love their homeland.

Before the Russian Revolution, most Russians were serfs who lived in villages and farmed the land owned by the upper classes. The serfs usually lived in village communes. Each family had a small wooden house painted in bright colors and decorated with elaborately carved wooden trim. Each house had a small kitchen garden for growing vegetables, herbs, and wild flowers for the family.

In these village communities, the heads of the households made the decisions for the good of the community. This strong group spirit still exists in daily Russian life today. Most Russians enjoy being in a group. They would even rather join a table of strangers in a restaurant than eat alone!

How Russians Live

Country Life versus City Life

Today, the small wooden houses in rural areas outside towns have a small kitchen garden, a few sunflowers, and a television antenna on the roof. Some homes still get their water from nearby wells, and many have their bathrooms outdoors.

In big cities, most Russians live in high-rise apartment buildings. A three-room apartment is standard size. Newer apartments have private baths and kitchens, but some people still live in older communal apartments where they share their bath or kitchen (or both) with another family. Housing in Russia has been limited since World War II, so several generations often live together in the same apartment.

Many urban families have a small plot of land in the country where they build a country house called a *dacha*. They will spend their weekends there and plant a garden to add to their food supply.

Leisure Time

On their days off, Russian families like to walk in the parks, see plays and movies, play sports, or just relax at home. In some of the larger cities, Russians can visit outstanding museums, such as the State Russian Museum in St. Petersburg, which houses the world's largest collection of Russian art.

In the spring and summer, many Russian families gather mushrooms in the woods around the cities. Even young kids are taught the difference between edible and poisonous mushrooms. This verse helps them to remember that the red cap, (or Death cap), mushroom is poisonous:

> In the pine forest, on the steep bank,
> Stands a little peasant in red cap.

Taking a Holiday

For people who *really* want to see Russia, the Trans-Siberian Railway is a great way to get a good look of about 6,000 miles of it. This is the longest rail line on earth and spans about one-third of the globe! Locals and tourists alike are now discovering the delight of watching the land race by, stopping in historic places along the way—and meeting other passengers. Remember: During train travel in Russia it is polite to share what you have with other people, including food and drink. So don't open a package of cookies without offering them to the people sitting near you!

For those who love the water, cruising on one of Russia's many rivers offers a great way to see the country from a different perspective. The Volga, for example, is 2,300 miles long and navigable over its entire length. A cruise on this longest river in Europe goes by some of Russia's most beautiful cities. Part of the fun is gliding by colorful medieval architecture that contrasts with the modern industrial buildings.

The Family Unit

Russian families are close—especially since two or three generations usually live together in a very small space! Most families have only one or two kids, and there are few stay-at-home moms. But even women who work outside the home are still responsible for household chores, grocery shopping, and childcare.

Naming the Kids

A Russian person's full name is composed of three names:

- A first name

- A middle name, which is a version of the father's first name formed by adding *vich* or *ovich* for a male and *avna* or *ovna* for a female. Thus, the son of Ivan would have a middle name of Ivanovich. The daughter of Ivan would have a middle name of Ivanovna. This middle name is called a *patronymic*.

- The family's last name

In formal situations, people use all three names. Acquaintances may refer to each other by their first and middle name. Close friends and family members call each other by first name only.

Common boys' names are Ivan, Vlad, Boris, Mikhail (Misha), or Alexander (Sasha, for short). Common girls' names are Masha (short for Maria), Natasha, Galina, Katya, or Sveta. Some names have special meanings. For example, Vera means faith.

Are We There Yet?

Life in the cities is extremely busy! Children may walk to school or ride with their parents on the Metro (the subway) or tram (streetcar). On the way home, mothers might stop to buy food, and there will probably be a line in front of the store of people waiting to get what they need.

Those who live in many parts of Siberia and the far eastern part of Russia still get around in horse-drawn sleighs! They might travel in dog sleds, too. Dog sled races are a part of many local festivities.

Going to School

Russia's population is almost entirely literate—something few other countries in the world have achieved. Education is free at all levels and guaranteed by law between ages seven and 17.

The educational system includes six-year primary schools and general, technical, or vocational secondary schools. In families where the mother works outside the home, the very young children may attend nursery school or kindergarten; or they might stay at home with the *babooshkas* (grandmothers).

Russian kids remain in the same class from Grade one through Grade 11 instead of getting new classmates each year. All school kids used to wear uniforms. They don't have to wear them anymore, but the school will still enforce a certain dress code that states what students can and cannot wear. Some private schools may require students to wear uniforms.

In the classroom, all students are expected to sit quietly at their desks, to stand when the teacher enters the room, and to stand when they are called on. Russian teachers are *very* strict. There's not much discussion between the teacher and the students. Kids listen to lectures and teachers point to students when they want answers. (This is even true at the university level.) First graders have a shorter school day than the older kids, but they still have to do homework!

Russian students generally don't take their lunch to school. They can buy a hot breakfast, snacks, and lunches at school, all for a very low price.

Some schools have class from Monday through Saturday. The kids start studying Russian, math, and science in Grade one and a foreign language around Grade four. In Grade two, some students go to special language schools to study a foreign language such as English, German, or French.

Most tests are given orally, but students take written exams at the end of each semester. After Grade eight and Grade 11, all students take comprehensive exams. They draw a question in each subject and recite their answer to a committee of teachers who decide if they will pass on to the next level.

After classes, the kids can stay at school until six PM. Many kids do, sitting with their friends to do homework or fun activities like dancing, singing, art, or sports. These after-school programs are free.

Students who want to pursue higher education will have lots of company—and *lots* of competition. The Russian Constitution guarantees a right to higher education in schools that are funded by the state. But getting admitted to one of these state-funded schools is tough. You have to be at the top of your class! The students who are admitted get free housing and a regular stipend (a payment used for living expenses).

Famous Russians

Many great writers, artists, athletes, scientists, musicians, composers, dancers, actors, architects, explorers, inventors, and scholars were born in Russia. Here are just a few of them.

Aleksandr Solzhenitsyn (sol-zha-neet-sen) (1918–2008) was one of the most famous Russians of the past fifty years. A novelist and historian, he made the world aware of the Soviet Union's forced labor camp system that imprisoned people who opposed the state. He was awarded the Nobel Prize in Literature in 1970 and was exiled from the Soviet Union in 1974; he returned to Russia in 1994.

Tennis star and model Anna Kournikova (1981–) has been ranked as the world's #1 doubles tennis player. Mikhail Baryshnikov (bar-ish-na-kof) (1948–) is the world's most widely recognized ballet dancer.

Name _____   Date _____

DESTINATION: MOSCOW!

Moscow is the capital of Russia *and* its largest city. It is filled with fun things to see and do. You have booked a five-day holiday in Moscow. Use the Internet and other resources to find out about each of the places written in your datebook. Write a few things you can expect to see at each place.

MONDAY
The Kremlin

TUESDAY
Pushkin Museum of Fine Arts

Roller-coaster at Gorky Park

WEDNESDAY
Gorky Park

THURSDAY
Moscow Zoo

FRIDAY
Great Moscow State Circus

Language & Expressions

Here are some fun facts about verbal and nonverbal communication in Russia.

Famous Russian Proverbs

Here are ten famous Russian proverbs. What do you think they mean?

A mere friend will agree with you, but a real friend will argue with you.

Don't raise your stick, and the dog won't bark at you.

Some people are masters of money, and some are its slaves.

The morning is wiser than the evening.

There is plenty of sound in an empty barrel.

When we sing, everybody hears us. When we sigh, nobody hears us.

A kind word is like a spring day.

Do not make an elephant out of a fly.

Every road has two directions.

Tell me who is your friend, and I'll tell you who you are.

Body Language and Etiquette in Russia

Here are some examples of body language and etiquette you'll find in Russia.

The typical greeting is an extremely firm handshake while maintaining direct eye contact and giving the greeting for the time of day (good morning, good afternoon, good evening).

Female friends greet by kissing on the cheek three times, starting with the left and then the right.

Close male friends may greet each other with a pat on the back and a hug.

Those invited to a Russian home for a meal are expected to bring a small gift. Male guests are expected to bring flowers—but not yellow flowers. And always give flowers in odd numbers. Giving an even number of flowers is only done for funerals.

It is bad luck to give a baby gift before the baby is born.

Guests are expected to arrive on time or no more than 15 minutes later than the invited time. Guests are expected to remove their outdoor shoes and may be given slippers to wear.

Always sit with the soles of your shoes facing the floor. Showing the soles of your shoes to a Russian is considered very disrespectful.

The oldest or most honored guest will be served first at a meal.

It is considered impolite to rest your elbows on the table during a meal. The hands should be visible at all times.

It is proper to leave a small amount of food on your plate. This tells your host that he or she has provided more than enough hospitality.

At formal dinners, the guest of honor is the first to get up from the table.

Single women should not sit at the corner of a table because this is considered bad luck.

If you visit Russia and you look like you're lost or need help, don't worry when several Russians surround you! Russians are eager to help!

Spitting over the left shoulder is thought to ward off bad luck. But whistling indoors is thought to bring bad luck!

Russian is written with the Cyrillic alphabet. It has thirty-three letters and is named after Saint Cyril, a Greek Orthodox monk. He and his brother, Saint Methodius, brought Christianity to the Slavic people in the ninth century CE. Many languages in Eastern Europe and Asia are written in the Cyrillic alphabet.

Below is the Cyrillic alphabet. Some letters probably look familiar to you! Some are pronounced like English. Some are not. Try to pronounce each letter!

Cyrillic letter   English letter or sound

А............A (ah)
Б............B (beh)
В............V (veh)
Г............G (geh)
Д............D (deh)
Е............E (yeh)
Ё............. (yoh)
Ж............J (zheh as in measure)
З............Z (zeh)
И............I (ee)
Й............Y (yih)
К............K (kah)
Л............L (elle)
М............M (em)
Н............N (en)
О............O (oh)

П............P (peh)
Р............R (err)
С............S (ess)
Т............T (teh)
У............oo
Ф............F (effe)
Х............k
Ц............ts
Ч............ch
Ш............sh
Щ............shch
Ъ............hard sign
Ы............i
Ь............soft sign
Э............eh
Ю............you
Я............yah

Know before You Go

Here are some common phrases you will use in Russia, along with the pronunciation. Try them out! Look up some additional ones!

English	Russian
Hello!	Preevyet!
Goodbye.	Dasveedanya.
How are you?	Yak dyela.
Good!	Hahrahsho.
Thanks.	Spaseeba.
My name is….	Menya zavoot….

Counting Numbers

Here are the Russian numbers from 1 to 10 with their pronunciations:

1	ОДИН	*adeen*	6	ШЕСТЬ	*shest*
2	ДВА	*dva*	7	СЕМЬ	*syem*
3	ТРИ	*tree*	8	ВОСЕМЬ	*vosyem*
4	ЧЕТЫРЕ	*chiteeree*	9	ДЕВЯТЬ	*devyat*
5	ПЯТЬ	*pyat*	10	ДЕСЯТЬ	*desyat*

FOODS

In most of northern Russia, the weather is cold and the growing season is limited. Soups and heavy dishes made of potatoes, noodles, and dairy products are popular here. In mountainous regions, dishes made of lamb or goat meat, fruits, and nuts are common. People gather many kinds of berries and mushrooms in the wooded regions to make tasty dishes, drinks, and desserts.

Russians often joke that they eat only once a day—but they eat one long meal that lasts for hours! This may be a bit of an exaggeration, but compared to weight-conscious Westerners who always seem to be watching their diets, Russians love to eat! They also love to entertain their guests with food. Visitors are always invited to eat something. If you are, be prepared for a long meal filled with well-seasoned dishes. Be prepared to try everything, too! It will be considered impolite if you don't.

Daily Meals

The big meal of the day is eaten in the mid-afternoon. Later, people will eat a light supper called *uzhim* that consists of hot tea and a pastry or roll filled with jam or cheese. They might have a light snack before bedtime, too.

Big meals start with *zakuski,* the appetizer, which may be small pieces of fish like herring or salmon in a sauce, or caviar on bread. Caviar is tiny, salty fish eggs that are usually black (from sturgeon) or red (from salmon). Stuffed hard-boiled eggs make good appetizers, as do *booterbrodi* (open-faced sandwiches).

The second course is always soup—hot or cold. The Russians make many kinds of vegetable and meat soups. *Shchi* is made from cabbage and has been served at Russian tables for more than a thousand years! *Borscht* is made from beets and beef. Small half-moon-shaped pies called *pirozhki* are filled with meat, potatoes, cheese, or cabbage. They are served with the soup, white bread, and heavy cream.

The third course is usually a chicken or meat dish with noodles, potatoes, or rice.

Finally, the meal ends with dessert. *Blini* are one of the most popular Russian desserts. They are wheat or buckwheat pancakes rolled around a filling and topped with a sauce, fruit preserves, or sour cream. (They are always served during the Russian Mardi Gras. *Blini* with caviar are a signature Russian dish.) Another favorite is *Charlotte Russe,* a cream-filled pastry topped with chocolate. Russian kids particularly like *pryaniki,* which are gingerbread cookies made in different shapes and glazed with icing.

Blini

The meal is rounded out with a few cups of black tea, the most popular national drink. Russia is one of the largest consumers of tea in the world.

Grabbing a Snack

In many of the larger Russian cities, it's easy to grab a snack from one of the many street vendors. You can get traditional items like blini, pirozhki, or sausage. Middle Eastern items like *shawerma* (a wrap sandwich of shaved meat like lamb or beef), rotisserie chicken, and skewers of meat are common, too. Chinese dishes are sold in areas with a high Chinese population. Even in this chilly country, ice cream is a popular favorite. So is pizza!

Holidays & Festivals

New Year • *January 1*

In the days before the Russian Revolution, people celebrated Christmas with as much enthusiasm as anywhere else in the world. Families decorated a *yolka* (pine tree), and kids rushed to see what gifts they had received from St. Nicholas on Christmas morning. In the country, the children dressed up in costume, going from house to house, singing and dancing in return for treats.

After the Revolution, the government forbade people to celebrate Christian holidays, so they transferred their Christmas customs to the New Year celebration, which is now a bigger holiday in Russia than Christmas. People still have their yolka and give gifts on New Year's Eve. Russian children sing this song as they circle around the yolka on New Year's Day:

> *A pine tree grew up in the wood,*
> *Deep in the woods it grew,*
> *All green and straight it stood,*
> *Both winter and summer, too.*

The children are told that Grandfather Frost delivered their gifts with the help of his assistant, Snow Maiden. Children in the cities often attend big yolka parties in youth clubs or even at the Kremlin, where they receive gifts and candy and watch clowns, acrobats, dancers, and skaters.

Russian Orthodox Christmas • *January 7*

Since 1992, Russian Orthodox Christmas is again being celebrated in Russia, and people have very much embraced the tradition. They go to an all-night Christmas Eve service filled with incense and candles. It's traditional to fast until after the service, when family members get together to celebrate. Meat is not permitted during the meal. Instead, *kutya* (koot-ya), a type of porridge, is the primary dish. It contains grains for hope and honey and poppy seeds for happiness and peace. Russians call this meal "The Holy Supper" in honor of the coming Christ Child. During the festive dinner that follows, all family members give thanks and express hope for the coming year.

Soldier's Day and Women's Day • *February 23 and March 8*

Soldier's Day is a holiday for all men, followed by Women's Day, which is a holiday for all women. On Soldier's Day, all men—particularly those who have served in the Russian military—are honored with good wishes and gifts. Women's Day is somewhat the same holiday for women, who receive gifts, flowers, and good wishes from the men in their lives.

Russian Orthodox Easter

Before the Russian Revolution, most of the holidays were holy days—that is, celebrations associated with the festivals of the Orthodox Church. The most important day for Orthodox Christians is Easter.

On Easter Eve, people cook, bake rich Easter cakes, and dye or paint Easter eggs. They then go to church in the late evening, taking their Easter breads and dyed eggs to be blessed by the priest. The worship service lasts all night. After the service, people exchange their dyed eggs, which are then sometimes used for egg rolling and other games.

Decorating Easter eggs reached its peak in Slavic countries like Russia. Here are some of the symbols used on the eggs:

Russian tsars, such as Alexander III and Nicholas II, had jeweled eggs of precious metals, enamel, and gemstones made for their families. These eggs opened to reveal tiny surprises inside. Created by Peter Carl Fabergé (fob-er-jay), these Imperial Easter Eggs are among the world's most treasured works of art. Of the 50 Imperial Easter Eggs created, only 42 have survived. Ten of them are displayed at the Kremlin Armoury Museum in Moscow. Thousands of smaller Faberge eggs were made by Fabergé from 1885 through 1917. These popular gifts were given during the Easter season.

May Day • *May 1*

May Day is now also known as Spring and Labor Day. When it occurs close to the Easter holiday, some people celebrate by going to church. Others attend parades and demonstrations in honor of workers. Workers themselves may march in parades.

Day of Victory • *May 9*

This is one of the biggest Russian holidays. It celebrates the Russian victory over Nazi Germany in World War II and honors the millions of Russians who died in that war. A military parade is held in Moscow each year and hosted by the President of the Russian Federation. Similar parades are held in other Russian cities. People put flowers and wreaths on the graves of the war's dead and attend demonstrations and parades. Surviving veterans (there are very few of them now) wear their military uniforms and medals and attend special concerts and parties in their honor. There is a fireworks display in the evening.

Russia Day • *June 12*

This is one of the newest Russian holidays, and it is also called Independence Day. It celebrates national unity and commemorates the adoption of the Declaration of Sovereignty of the Russian Federation in 1991.

Unity Day • *November 4*

Russia's newest holiday, first celebrated in 2005, commemorates an uprising that drove Polish invaders from Moscow in 1612 and ended foreign occupation in Russia. The name of the holiday symbolizes the idea that all classes of Russian society united to save Russia. Many people think of this as a replacement for a former holiday on November 7 that marked the anniversary of the Bolshevik Revolution.

Name _____   Date _____

MAKE A FABERGÉ EGG

Fabergé eggs are among the world's greatest decorative arts. These priceless treasures were made of precious metals, enamel, and gemstones. Make your own Fabergé egg!

Materials
- Glue
- Scissors
- Pencil
- Paper plate or stiff piece of cardboard
- Items of your choice: sequins, glitter, ribbons, small artificial gems or pearls, paint

Directions
1. Trace the egg template below onto a paper plate or stiff piece of cardboard and cut it out.

2. Decorate the egg however you choose! You can use one of these patterns or create your own.

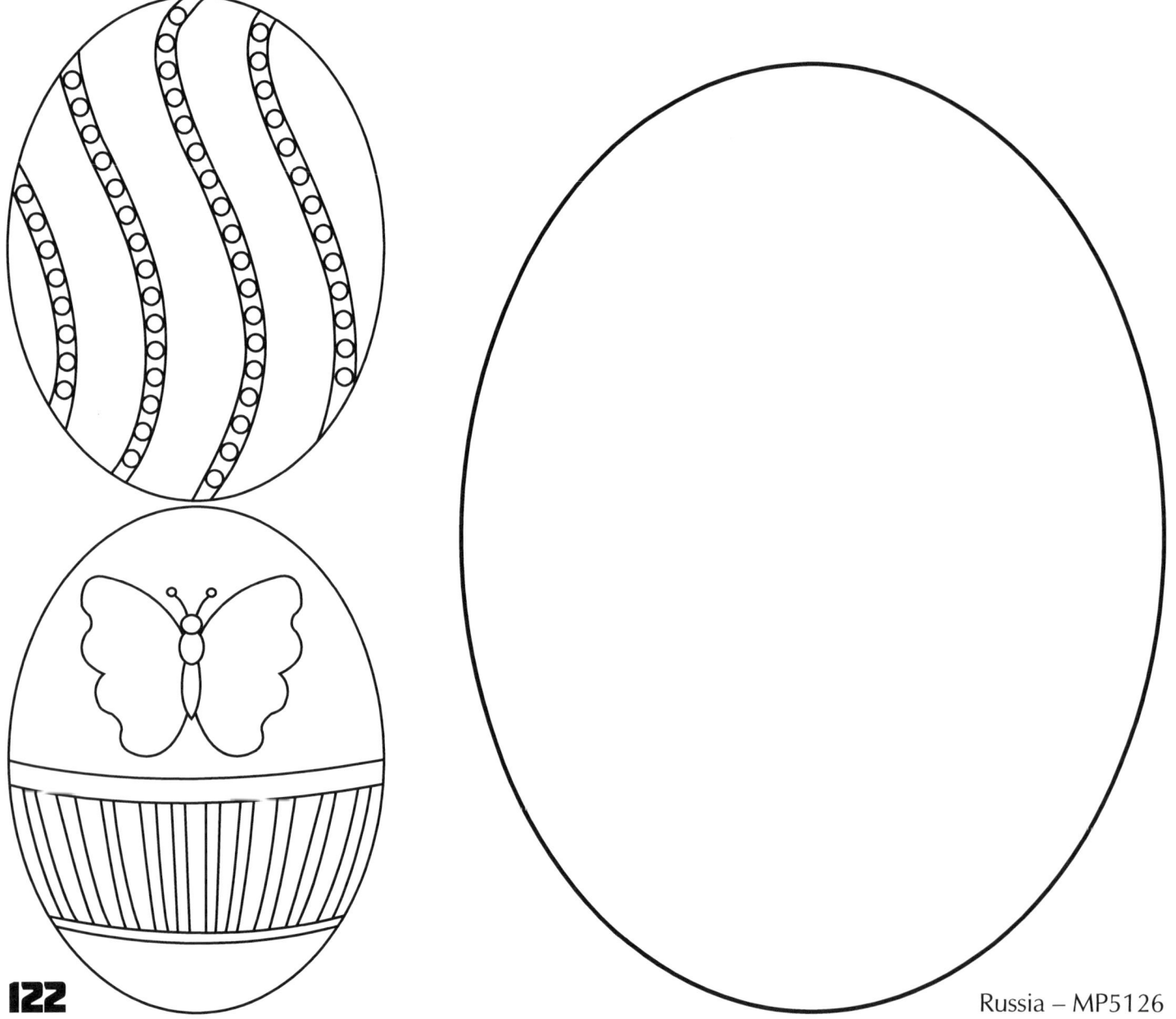

Russia – MP5126

Creative Arts

Music and Dance

Russian music and dance are among the best in the world. That's no surprise! Russia's musicians and dancers (like its athletes) begin training before they even begin grade school. Preschool kids who show talent in music and dance study intensively for many years. Students who get to perform in one of Russia's ballet companies or one of its symphonies have made it to the top. Many of the world's finest ballet dancers, such as Mikhail Baryshnikov, Alexander Godunov, Rudolf Nureyev, and Natalia Makarova, were born and trained in Russia. Russia's Bolshoi Ballet in Moscow and Kirov Ballet in St. Petersburg are two of the finest ballet companies in the world.

One of the greatest Russian ballet dancers was Anna Pavlova. She was born in St. Petersburg in 1881. She later toured the world with her own company, dancing her favorite roles in *Giselle*, *The Sleeping Beauty*, and *Swan Lake*.

Peter Ilyich Tchaikovsky (chī-kof-skee) wrote the music for both *Swan Lake* and *The Sleeping Beauty*. He also composed *The Nutcracker* ballet that is often performed during the holiday season. A musical work that both children and adults love is *Peter and the Wolf* by Sergei Prokofiev. It tells the story of a boy who kills a wolf with the help of his animal friends. Each character in the story is represented by a different instrument.

Russian folk dances are colorful, fun to watch, and fun to do! Russian children go to special classes after school to learn how to do the old folk dances. These dances depict village life and customs, such as exciting sleigh rides behind a *troika*—a team of three horses pulling a sleigh.

Folk Art

Enameled plates, spoons, mugs, and bowls with golden leaves and red berries on a black or gold background were originally crafted in the town of Khokhloma. *Khokhloma ware* is especially popular with tourists, as are the black lacquered boxes, trays, and jewelry produced in the town of Palekh. These are often decorated with scenes from Russian fairy tales and have become prized possessions.

Folk Tales and Fairy Tales

Popular Characters

Russian culture is rich with *folk tales* (tales passed down through the generations by word of mouth) and *fairy tales* (stories with magical creatures). Russian children learn many of these wonderful stories, filled with witches, animals, and magical events. Here are some of the most popular characters from Russian folk tales and fairy tales.

> *Baba Yaga* is an old witch who lives in a house that stands on chicken legs in the forest. She captures children and makes them serve her. *Vasilisa the Beautiful* is a girl sent to the woods and taken captive by Baba Yaga. This story is similar to the fairy tale *Hansel and Gretel*.

Sister Alyonushka and Brother Ivanushka is the story of a brother and sister who remain loyal to each other despite many troubles.

There are many stories with heroes named *Ivan*. In most of these, the young boy must fulfill three tasks in order to win fame, fortune, or the love of a beautiful girl.

Animals in Folk Tales and Fairy Tales

Many animals appear in Russian folk tales and fairy tales. They have their roots in early Russian history and have great meaning for modern Russians as well.

The bear symbolizes strength, power, warmth, and protection. It is Russia's most beloved animal. Its Russian name, *med'ved,* means *one who knows where the honey is*. Early Slavic foresters survived the long winters with the bear's coat for warmth and meat for food. From this, a myth of the bear as an ancestor of the people developed. It appears in many folk tales, often as a wise old man of the woods, commonly named Mikhail or Misha. A little brown bear named Misha was the mascot of the 1980 Summer Olympic Games in Moscow.

The rooster appears not only in folk tales and fairy tales, but also on folk items such as toys, towels, plates, clothing, and teapots. Russians associate the rooster with the sun and good fortune. Two roosters with their heads together often appear on wedding gifts to wish the bride and groom a happy marriage. In folk tales, magic hens lay golden eggs and make their owners rich. Alexander Pushkin, one of Russia's great poets, wrote "The Tale of the Golden Cockerel," in which a rooster warns the tsar whenever there is a sign of unrest on the country's borders.

The horse was important to early Slavs for transportation. It is also associated with the mythical winged horse that pulled the sun back and forth across the sky. Magical horses appear in Russian fairy tales, like "The Little Humpbacked Horse" by Pyotr (pā-ter) Pavlovich Yershov.

Folk Costumes

Although Russians now dress pretty much the same way people do in the West, dancers and musicians sometimes still wear the beautiful Russian folk costumes during performances.

Sarafan and Kokoshnik

A *sarafan* is a long jumper-style dress that peasant girls and women in central and northern Russia wore until well into the 20th century. The sarafan can be simple black fabric or have elaborate embroidery of brocade or silk. Sometimes a corset is worn over the dress. A white blouse was worn underneath it.

The *kokoshnik* is traditionally worn with the sarafan. This tiara-like, ceremonial headdress can be pointed or round; it was usually heavily beaded. The long ribbons on this headdress are tied at the back of the head in a large bow. The woman or girl wearing this kokoshnik usually has her hair in braids.

Kosovorotka

Like the sarafan, the kosovorotka is generally associated with Russian peasants and was worn until well into the 20th century. This long-sleeved shirt reaches down to the mid-thigh and is belted at the waist. It is not tucked into the trousers. The shirt has several buttons at the collar.

Kosovorotka

DANCE THE TROIKA!

The *troika* is a popular dance in Russia. All you need is some Russian folk music, a space big enough to dance in, and several other people. The more people you have, the more fun it is! Follow these simple steps.

1. Form several groups with two or three others. Each group should hold hands.

2. Walk or skip forward together eight steps to the music, holding hands.

3. Walk or skip backward together eight steps, still holding hands.

4. Circle once to the left for five steps.

5. Stop and stamp your feet three times.

6. Circle again to the left for five more steps.

7. Stop and stamp your feet three times.

8. Repeat these simple steps from the beginning as many times as you like!

Sports & Games

Sports

Russians have excelled in sports for decades. Like the kids who show talent in music and dance, kids who have athletic ability are trained from a very early age. As a result, Russians consistently win medals at the Olympic Games and other international competitions. Russian gymnasts, track-and-field athletes, weight lifters, wrestlers, figure skaters, skiers, and many others continue to be among the best in the world. Since 1952, they have been among the top three nations collecting the most gold medals at the Summer Olympic Games.

Winter sports are extremely popular in the very cold land of Russia! Most children in Moscow and in the north learn to ski and skate in early grade school. Sledding and building snowmen are favorite activities for the young and the old. The large Russian *sanki* (sled), pulled by three horses (a troika), has been the inspiration for many paintings, songs, and even a folk dance. In the summer, many children spend a month or more at a youth camp where they learn crafts and sports.

Russians also love ball games like football (soccer). An old Russian game called *lapta* is played with a small bat and ball, somewhat like baseball. The players divide into two teams and take turns pitching, batting, and running along a straight line across the field and back.

Games

Russian kids have similar versions of many of the games other kids play, like *klassiki* (hopscotch), *preeyatki* (hide-and-seek), *salki* (tag), and *chekardi* (leapfrog).

Russians of all ages enjoy board games like dominoes, checkers, and chess. Chess, in fact, has the status of an official sport in Russia, and even young children play it. There are many chess clubs and competitions in Russia. People also enjoy putting together puzzles and models.

Favorite Toys

Russian kids grow up with toys that have been loved by generations of Russian children, such as wooden toys, dolls, and puppets. One toy perhaps most associated with Russia is the little mother nesting dolls called *matryoshka* (ma-tree-osh-ka). These dolls may have begun as nesting eggs. Some of them have as many as fifteen or twenty dolls nested inside each other! Even today, they are considered a symbol of motherhood.

Other traditional toys are clay animal whistles worn around the neck on a string. The brightly painted roosters, horses, or other animals are made to resemble creatures from popular fairy tales.

matryoshka, or little mother nesting dolls

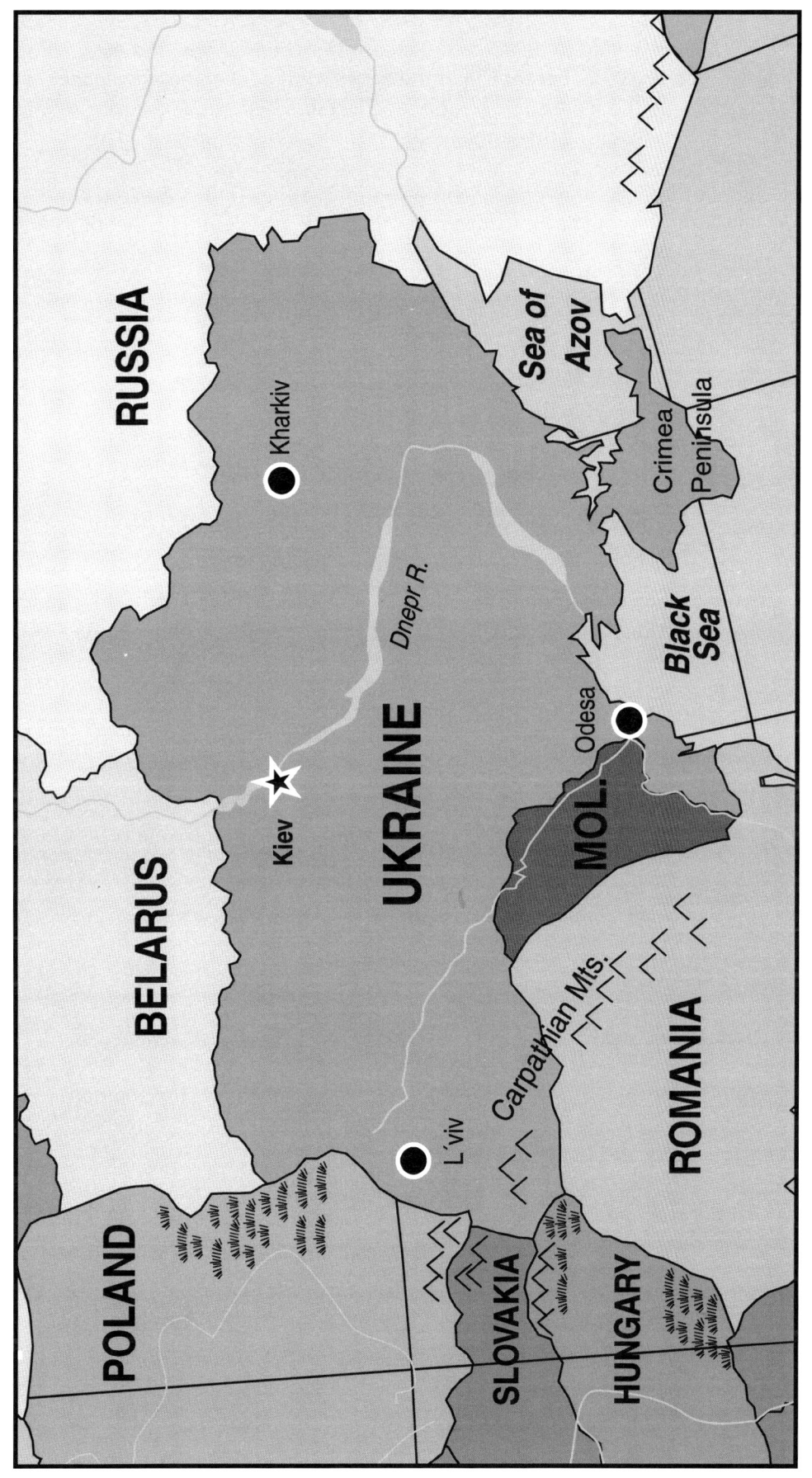

WELCOME TO UKRAINE!

Ukraine, which means *borderland*, is said to be at the crossroads between Europe and Asia. Europe's second largest country, it became independent in 1991 after the fall of the Soviet Union. Ukraine now leads a sort of double life as an old and yet new country. On the west is Europe, helping Ukraine become Westernized. On the east is Russia, with whom it shares a long history, assuring that it maintains a strong connection to its past.

Like many former Soviet countries, Ukraine remains somewhat mysterious to the Western world. But an increasing number of tourists are slowly discovering its incredible natural beauty. The country is steadily carving out its own unique identity in the 21st century.

FAST FACTS

Official Name:	Ukraine
Location:	Eastern Europe, bordering the Black Sea, between Poland, Romania, and Moldova in the west, and Russia in the east. Ukraine is at the crossroads between Asia and Europe. It is the second largest country in Europe.
Population:	45,700,395 (2010 estimate)
Capital City:	Kiev
Area:	233,090 square miles. Ukraine is slightly smaller than the state of Texas.
Major Language:	Ukrainian (the official language): 67% Russian: 24%
Major Religion:	Ukrainian Orthodox
Currency:	hryvnya (riv-nya) 1 hryvnya = 100 kopiykas (ko-pē-kas)
Climate:	Generally temperate with a Mediterranean climate along the southern Crimean coast. Winters are cool along the Black Sea and cold farther inland. Summers are warm across most of the country and hot in the south.
The Land:	Mostly forest, forest steppes, steppes, and plateaus. Mountains are found in the west (the Carpathians) and in the Crimean Peninsula in the extreme south.
Type of Government:	Republic
Flag:	Two equal horizontal bands of azure (at the top) and golden yellow (at the bottom). The colors represent grain fields under a blue sky.

Coat of Arms:	Commonly called the Tryzub (trī-zoob), Ukraine's national Coat of Arms features the same colors as the flag. The blue shield has a yellow trident (three-pronged spear), called a tryzub. Most historians think the trident is a stylized image of a hawk.
National Flower:	Sunflower (Helianthus annuus)
National Tree:	Viburnum

Natural Environment

Ukraine is a gem of natural beauty. It consists of forests and steppes (plains of natural grassland) crossed by several rivers that flow south into the Black Sea and the Sea of Azov. Almost all the Ukrainian steppe and large areas of the forest are now being farmed. A network of natural preserves and national parks in Ukraine are carefully maintained to protect the environment.

There are only two mountain ranges in Ukraine. The Carpathian Mountains in the west include Hoverla Mountain, the highest in the country at 6,670 feet. The mountains on the Crimean Peninsula in the southern portion of the country run along the coast.

The Carpathian Mountains are known and loved throughout Europe. The mineral springs, healthy climate, and unique flora and fauna make them a prime resort and recreation area. Each region of the Carpathians has its own incredible charm, from tiny villages tucked into the green folds of the mountainside to lush forest reserves and national parks. The World Wildlife Fund has recognized the Carpathians as a global treasure and one of the Earth's most significant ecosystems.

The Crimean Mountains consist of cliffs and caves above and below water. The Crimean southern shore is the key resort and tourist area of Ukraine and one of the most important ones in Eastern Europe. Tourists enjoy the mild climate, soak in the healing water *and* the healing mud, and take in the natural beauty.

The Dnieper (nee-per) River is the largest in Ukraine and the third largest in Europe, after the Volga and the Danube. The Ukrainian capital of Kiev is located on the Dnieper. The Dniester (nees-ter) River, the second largest in Ukraine, flows close to the border of Poland and to the Black Sea. In addition to these rivers, there are thousands of smaller ones in Ukraine, most of which flow south into the Black Sea or the Sea of Azov. The coasts of both the Black Sea and the Sea of Azov form the boundary of the Ukrainian territories in the south.

Dnieper River

Plants and Animals

The dense, green forests of western and southern Ukraine cover an extensive area and are rich with fir, spruce, beech, and ash trees. The forest steppe is a gently rolling central plain covered with thick, low vegetation. It is now being heavily cultivated with crops such as wheat and corn. The creatures you'll find here include squirrels, rabbits, bobcats, foxes, deer, and even otters, along with woodpeckers, pigeons, and turtledoves.

Like the forest steppes, the central steppes are being heavily cultivated with hay, grain, sugar beets, and sunflowers. Sheep graze in the dry pastures. But, for the most part, the animals of the steppes are soil-boring rodents, such as rabbits, mice, and rats, who are trying to hide from predators like the fox, wolf, and polecat.

In the beautiful Black Sea to the south of Ukraine you'll find dolphins, rare white-bellied seals, and many species of smaller sea creatures like the sea horse. In the Sea of Azov to the southeast you'll find similar varieties of fish found in the Black Sea, along with Azov herring and anchovies.

Medicinal Plants

In Ukraine, there are about 1,200 species of medicinal plants, like juniper and yarrow, which are used to make medicines, teas, juices, and powders to help cure illness in humans and animals. Medicinal plants play a starring role in many Ukrainian folk songs and folk tales. Throughout Ukraine's long history, people who knew how to use these plants were given special status.

A History of Ukraine

The oldest traces of human existence in Ukraine go back to the Stone Age. By 40,000–15,000 BCE, almost all of Ukraine was inhabited by clans of hunters and gatherers who farmed, made their own everyday items, and lived peacefully. By 4500 BCE, there were settlements throughout the land.

Between 700 and 200 BCE, Ukraine was part of the Scythian Kingdom. Beginning in the sixth century BCE, colonies of Ancient Greece, Ancient Rome, and the Byzantine Empire were founded on the northeastern shore of the Black Sea and thrived well into the sixth century CE.

Modern History

The modern history of Ukraine begins in the ninth century, when it was the center of the East Slavs who became the Russian, Ukrainian, and Belarusian people by the 17th century. This state, called Kievan Rus', became the largest and most powerful nation in Europe before it dissolved in the 12th century because of in-fighting and invasions. Kievan Rus' was incorporated into the Grand Duchy of Lithuania and eventually into the Polish-Lithuanian Commonwealth. The culture and religion of the Kievan Rus', however, laid the foundation for Ukrainian culture and religion.

As a result of the Great Northern War (1700–1721), Russia gained control of the Baltic Sea and became a major power in Europe. By the 19th century, most of Ukraine was absorbed into the Russian Empire.

Ukraine under Stalin

Ukraine endured years of fighting and hardship. It tried several times to become independent following World War I (1914–1918) and the Russian Civil War (1917–1923). It did enjoy a few years of independence from 1917 to 1920. But Russia regained control of it. In 1922, it became one of the founding republics of the Soviet Union and was officially called the Ukrainian Soviet Socialist Republic.

Joseph Stalin was a brutal leader of the Soviet Union. He abolished private industry and nationalized all businesses so they were under government control. The peasant farmers were put on collective farms and given impossible quotas to fill. The farmers themselves were not allowed to receive grain until they met their quotas. Those who refused to participate in this state-run program were killed, put in concentration camps, or shipped off to Siberia or the Arctic. As a result of Stalin's policies, Ukraine endured two famines in which more than eight million people died—during 1921–1922 and 1932–1933. Ironically, Ukraine had always been considered the "breadbasket" of the Soviet Union.

In 1933, Stalin officially declared that all elements of Ukrainian life were to be abolished so the country could become entirely Russian. Ukrainian society and culture were violently changed. Four-fifths of Ukrainian intellectuals, artists, and other cultural leaders were killed. The Ukrainian political leaders disappeared.

World War II

Ukraine continued to suffer tremendously during the Nazi occupation of the country from 1941 to 1944. More than five million Ukrainians died fighting the Nazis. Most of Ukraine's 1.5 million Jews died at the hands of the Nazis as well.

Stalin accused the Crimean Tatars, an ethnic group living in Crimea, of collaborating with the Nazis. In 1944, he deported about 200,000 of them to Central Asia. Since the late 1980s, more than 250,000 of them have returned to Crimea.

Rebuilding after the War

World War II devastated Ukraine, as it did much of Europe. Ukraine lost 700 of its cities and towns, and 28,000 of its villages. Despite this, Ukraine became one of the founding members of the United Nations in 1945.

Following Stalin's death in 1953, Nikita Khrushchev (kru-shev) became the new leader of the Soviet Union. Ukraine began to rebuild. It gained Crimea from Russia in 1954. Today, Crimea is an autonomous republic on the northern coast of the Black Sea that also occupies a peninsula. The Russian Black Sea Fleet is still based there.

The Soviets invested heavily in Ukraine and greatly increased its industry and workforce. The Ukrainian economy eventually became the second largest in the Soviet Union! Many people who became leaders of the Soviet Union came from Ukraine, as well as athletes, artists, and scientists.

Chernobyl

In 1986, a reactor at the Chernobyl (shāre-nō-bul) Nuclear Power Plant in northern Ukraine exploded, causing the worst nuclear reactor accident in history. Of the 7.7 million people who lived in contaminated territory, 2.2 million of them were in Ukraine. The radiation from the accident contaminated about eight percent of Ukraine's territory. Many people continue to suffer from the aftereffects of the radiation exposure.

Independence—Once Again!

After the collapse of the Soviet Union in 1991, Ukraine became an independent nation again. But with independence came hardship. Ukraine's first president after independence, former Communist Party official Leonid Kravchuk, came to office during a period with a seriously bad economy and inflation. Many Ukrainians organized strikes and protested the terrible conditions.

Life continued to be a struggle, but Ukrainians pressed on. People in the countryside survived by growing their own food, while people in the cities survived by working several jobs.

Ukraine under Yushchenko

Viktor Yushchenko (Yu-shenk-ō) became Ukraine's third president in 2005. His road to the presidency was difficult, and his time in office has been difficult, too. Yushchenko was declared the loser in the presidential elections of 2004. He and thousands of his supporters staged protests, declaring that the election was rigged. After ten days of demonstrations, called the Orange Revolution because the protestors wore orange, Yushchenko won a new election.

Although Yushchenko wants to reform and Westernize Ukraine, the world economy has been tough on the country. Ukraine depends on its steel exports, but the global financial crisis of 2008 heavily affected its steel industry. In the fall of 2008, Ukraine received a $16.5 billion loan from the International Monetary Fund to help boost its economy.

Russia is still a key trading partner, but this has proved to be a tough relationship. Ukraine gets about 35 percent of its natural gas supply from Russia and is part of the pipeline for 85 percent of the Russian gas exported to Europe. Russia briefly cut its gas supplies to Ukraine in 2006 and 2009—which caused gas shortages not only in Ukraine, but in other European countries.

One of Yushchenko's key campaign promises was to fight corruption, but he himself has been accused of it. Despite his extremely low ratings in the opinion polls, he wants to continue as president. He continues to propose major government reforms. He is still seeking NATO membership, which would strengthen Ukraine's defenses if attacked. He continues to push for Ukraine to become a member of the European Union, possibly by 2015.

Ukraine Rockets into the Future

Today, Ukraine is looking forward. It is a world leader in producing missiles and missile-related technology. It participates in space exploration programs and maintains its own space agency. It also ranks high in the number of tourists visiting annually!

For a country with such a difficult and unhappy past, Ukraine continues to build for a happier future. It will co-host the European Football Championships in 2012 and may even get a shot at hosting the 2018 Winter Olympic Games. Once hidden from view, Ukraine is slowly and steadily showing its best face to the world. And what a fascinating face it is!

Daily Life

So Long Soviet Past!

Freedom of Speech

Until the late 20th century, Ukraine still identified with its Soviet past. Today, Ukrainians are becoming very much like people in the West, thanks to their increasing knowledge of European culture. They're speaking up, speaking out, and dressing and acting the part of people in a free society.

During the Soviet era, disagreement with the government's policies—at least in public—was never allowed. Ukrainians now have freedom of speech and freedom to express themselves, and they're doing both on a daily basis. For the most part, the government no longer controls the media. It's not uncommon to hear, see, and read criticism of the government on TV and radio, and in newspapers and magazines. Voters now feel that they can choose candidates and decide on issues. It appears that fixed national elections are a thing of the past. However, some employers demand that their employees vote a certain way in local elections.

Freedom of Expression

If you were judging on clothing alone, it might be hard to tell an urban Ukrainian from an urban American these days. In the Soviet era, everyone was expected to dress the same—usually in gray, brown, and black—and not stand out. Today, the opposite is true. Students especially dress the way they want—and it usually involves wearing jeans!

Big retail stores are offering a host of cool stuff—and people are buying. The spending may not have reached the level of "shop til you drop." But Ukrainians—especially in big cities like Kiev—are now able to buy at least some of the clothing, sporting goods, jewelry, and other items available in Europe. And they love it! More shopping centers are popping up all the time.

Home and Family

City Life versus Country Life

Kiev

In America, it's common for people to move to other neighborhoods, other states, and even other countries. In Ukraine, people tend to stay where they were brought up. Since the country was once mostly a farming society, most people have relatives in the country. The population of the cities is increasing all the time, however.

City-dwellers often live in small apartments in high-rise buildings. Private homes are becoming more common. There's the typical hustle and bustle you'd expect in any large city—lots of people walking, cycling, or taking public transportation. Smaller Ukrainian towns are more charming, with quaint old buildings and a central square. The much smaller villages are still fairly isolated from the outside world. People live in small houses that they go to great lengths to decorate. They work in community-owned fields and come home to a traditional family life at night, capped off by an evening of watching TV as a family.

Family Roles

Whether in the city or in the country, grandparents help raise their grandchildren. They may even live with them. There is definitely a standard of behavior for kids of all ages. They're expected to keep out of trouble and do well in school. They're also expected to behave in public.

Men and women still tend to have traditional roles. The wife does the cooking and cleaning, while the husband takes care of home repairs. This is changing as Ukraine becomes more exposed to Western society. Today, young people getting married can expect to split the household chores and do the ones they like. It's not uncommon for men to do all the cooking in some homes!

Kickin' Back

What Ukrainians do in their free time has much to do with their beautiful environment. Strolling and cycling in a park are fun pastimes. Spending a few hours picnicking in one of the parks, nature reserves, or in one of the beautiful resort areas is another way to enjoy time off. With so many lakes and rivers close to so many of the cities and towns, Ukrainians are avid swimmers. A few brave souls even do polar bear dives in the freezing water on winter days. Since Ukrainians can now get better sporting goods, they're turning to sports that require better gear—like bungee jumping.

National Kindness

Friendships really mean something to Ukrainians, and they form them easily. Think of how the word *friend* is used in America. It probably means someone you know, but it doesn't necessarily mean someone you know *well*.

In Ukraine, people have one or two friends (*really* close friends they know well) and few or several acquaintances. Ukrainians love to get together to talk and enjoy each other's company. They care about each other's opinions. And they share lots of activities, like hobby groups. Sometimes the activity groups are just an excuse to get together and hang out!

This national kindness even extends to the workplace. Employees celebrate their own birthdays at work by bringing treats or even entire meals for everyone in the office. Companies give birthday gifts to their employees.

Going to School

The Ukrainian constitution gives all citizens access to free education. Most of the schools in Ukraine are state-run, though there are some private secondary schools and higher-education institutions.

By law, students must go to school for twelve years. Primary school education starts at age six and takes four years to complete. Middle (also called secondary) education takes five years to complete. Upper secondary education takes three years. In the 12th grade, students take government tests called school-leaving exams that determine which students get into university.

Good behavior while in school is not an option—it's a requirement! Other kids might see teachers as friends. But Ukrainian kids see them as stern authority figures who do not allow disobedience. Students remain respectful of teachers and address them as honored individuals.

In many countries, sports and other activities encourage kids to be competitive and cause them to spend time away from home after school. There are few such extracurricular activities in Ukrainian schools, so kids generally stay home a lot more.

Famous People from Ukraine

Actress, model, and singer-songwriter Milla Jovovich (1975–) was born in Kiev. Many Soviet politicians and revolutionaries came from Ukraine. These include Leon Trotsky, one of the most famous leaders of the Russian Revolution, and Leonid Brezhnev (1906–1982), the leader of the Soviet Union from 1964–1982.

Oksana Baiul (bī-ule) (1977–) is a professional figure skater. A 1994 Olympic gold medalist, she beat the American favorite for the gold medal, Nancy Kerrigan, by only 0.1 points.

Here are some fun facts about verbal and nonverbal communication in Ukraine.

Famous Ukrainian Proverbs

Here are five famous Ukrainian proverbs. What do you think they mean?

He is guilty who is not at home.
Your head is not only for putting a hat on.
Only when you have eaten a lemon do you appreciate what sugar is.
Every disadvantage has its advantage.
No matter how hard you try, the bull will never give milk.

Body Language and Etiquette in Ukraine

Here are some examples of body language and etiquette you'll find in Ukraine.

If you are a house guest in a Ukrainian home, you'll get more than food. Your guest will probably take you around to see the sights!

Ice water is thought to cause colds, so you probably won't be offered a glass of ice water at a meal, or any other time.

While Americans tend to stand a good arm's length apart, Ukrainians stand a bit closer to each other during conversation. They may even touch each other quite a bit. They do not use large gestures, however.

It's considered okay to greet a woman with a kiss on the cheek.

People are generally formal in public. They also do not generally smile on the street. Smiles are reserved for personal relationships.

Although people generally laugh about superstitions, they don't break them! So, they won't do things that are thought to bring back luck, such as shake hands through a doorway or whistle indoors.

Know before You Go

Both Ukrainian and Russian are spoken in Ukraine. In some of the larger cities like Kiev, signs will be in both Russian and Ukrainian. For some common Russian phrases, see page 118. Here are some common phrases you will use in Ukraine, along with the pronunciations. Try them out! Look up some additional ones!

English	Ukrainian	Pronunciation
Hello.	Vitayu.	vee-tī-u
Goodbye.	Do pobachennya.	dō pō-bach-een-ya
Good morning.	Dobrogo rankoo.	dō-bra-hō ran-kō
Good afternoon.	Dobrogo dnia'.	dō-bra-hō nee'a
Good evening.	Dobryy' vechar.	dō-brī vā-cher
Good night.	Dobranich.	dō-bra-neech
Yes.	Tak.	tak
No.	Ni.	nī
Thank you.	Dyakuyu.	yak-u-yu
You're welcome.	Proshu, bud' laska.	pro-shoo bood-las-ka
How are you?	Jak sia majete?	yok-see-a my-et-ā

FOODS

Ukrainian food is similar to that of its neighbors, Europe and Russia. Like its neighbors, food figures heavily into celebrations of any kind. The food is rich, delicious, and filling. It's usually well seasoned with local herbs, such as chives, dill, caraway seeds, and parsley.

Bread, Baked Goods, and Other Doughy Delights

Since ancient times, bread has been a cornerstone of Ukrainian cuisine. Sour rye bread is on the table every day. But Ukrainians bake special loaves for special occasions. Braided bread *(kalach)*, Easter bread *(paska)*, bread with a filling, wedding bread *(korovai)*, sweet bread *(babka)*, and egg bread *(bulka)* are among them. Every special event—the harvest, marriage, birth of a child, moving to a new home, a funeral—is marked with a special bread that has its own meaning. Guests are greeted with bread and salt to show hospitality. Easter bread, decorated with dough ornaments, is brought to the church to be blessed.

All sorts of baked goods fill the Ukrainian table at any time of day. Turnovers, pies, doughnuts, strudel, poppy seed rolls, buns, tortes, layered coffee cakes, honey cake, cookies, and cheesecake are part of the daily fare. *Pampushky* (pam-poosh-kē), similar to doughnut holes, are tossed with delicious cinnamon sugar and are often stuffed with sweet fillings.

Dishes made of dough are popular, too. *Zatyrka* (za-teer-ka), for example, consists of pieces of dough dropped into boiling water or milk. Dumplings are made with various fillings, including cheese, potato, cabbage, meat, fish, buckwheat, and plum. One quick dish is made of dough cut into triangles and sometimes served with bacon, fried onions, or sour cream. Egg noodles are served with soup or cheese.

Meat and Fish

Meat is common in the Ukrainian diet, and the most popular is pork. This includes ham, sausage, smoked bacon, and salt pork. Potatoes, cabbage, and mushrooms are often served with meat. Chicken is often served baked in sour cream, stuffed, roasted, fried, or boiled in soup.

Fish is served several ways, both hot and cold. It's fried, poached, or baked with dressing. It's also jellied, deep fried in fritters, marinated, and smoked. Salted herring is a centuries-old cold appetizer.

Potatoes, Cabbage, and Other Veggies

Like bread, the potato is a cornerstone of Ukrainian cooking. You'll find it in soups. It's baked or broiled and served along or with meats, fish, cheese, cabbage, and other vegetables. Shredded potatoes are formed into pancakes, fried, and served with cheese or sour cream. Some dumplings are filled with potatoes.

Cabbage, particularly sauerkraut, is used to make cabbage soup or is served with meat, pea puree, or potatoes. Fresh cabbage leaves serve as the veggie "jackets" for cabbage rolls, which are stuffed with rice and meat.

Ukrainians eat onions, garlic, carrots, turnips, radishes, and cucumbers raw as appetizers or tasty snacks. Roasted sunflower and pumpkin seeds are popular. People preserve cucumbers, cabbage, tomatoes, and beets. Peas and beans seasoned with garlic or fried bacon, tomatoes used as appetizers or in borsch, and many types of mushrooms round out the veggie menu.

Borscht

Borscht is a popular soup in many Eastern European countries, and Ukraine is no exception! Dinner traditionally starts with a soup, and it's often borscht. It includes vegetables (particularly beets and cabbage) and meat stock or fish stock. At Christmas, people eat meatless borscht. At any time of year, it's served with sour cream or rye bread. Each region has its own tasty borscht recipe.

Fruits

Ukrainians eat berries and other fruit fresh or cooked into thick purees and compotes. Plum butter is great on a thick piece of bread. Fruits like apples are dried or preserved for the winter. Jellied fruits like cherries are popular, too.

Beverages

Soured milk is a favorite drink in Ukraine, similar to the buttermilk people drink in other countries. Bread *kvas* (a drink actually made from bread that has a sour taste), fruit or dill-pickle brine, and birch sap are popular beverages in the countryside. (The birch sap does actually come from the birch tree the way syrup comes from a maple tree.) Tea, coffee, and cocoa are the most popular hot drinks.

Holidays & Festivals

New Year's Day • *January 1*

As with other Eastern European countries, New Year's is far and away the key holiday and the national favorite. People wait for New Year in Ukraine like others anticipate Christmas, Hanukkah, or Kwanza. Tree decorating, cooking and baking, buying presents, and partying from late December into early January are just some of the things that people look forward to. According to an old saying, people spend the new year the way they welcome it. So everyone is up for having some fun with family and friends. Kids look forward to the gifts brought by Santa Claus (called *Ded Moroz*) on New Year's Eve.

Orthodox Christmas • *January 7*

The Soviets did not celebrate Christmas, but since the country's independence, Ukrainians are once again enjoying this peaceful and happy religious holiday. On Christmas Eve, families eat a 12-course meal to remind them of Christ's 12 apostles. The meal includes *kutia* (ku-tī-a) (bread with honey and red poppies), borscht, dumplings stuffed with vegetables and potatoes, fish, and stuffed cabbage. In recent years, people have been reviving old Christmas traditions, such as masked kids going door to door to get candy in exchange for singing Christmas carols.

Valentine's Day • *February 14*

Valentine's Day is originally a European and American holiday, but Ukrainians love celebrating it, too! And they do it in pretty much the same way people in other parts of the world do. They exchange cards with loving messages, give flowers and candy, and have a special meal at home or in a restaurant.

Women's Day • *March 8*

This popular holiday was originally introduced by the Soviet Communists. Gender roles are still traditional in Ukraine, and women still do much of the housework and child care. So on this day, men are expected to do everything around the house, like cleaning, cooking, and watching the kids. They're also expected to give their wives, sweethearts, mothers, daughters, sisters, friends, and female coworkers tokens of appreciation like candy and flowers.

Orthodox Easter • *About Two Weeks after Catholic Easter*

This is the major religious holiday in the Orthodox Church. People prepare for it for weeks and enjoy it enormously when it comes. On Easter Eve, people attend church for a festive, happy service in which the priest blesses the *kulichi* (Easter cake) and *pysanki* (painted Easter eggs)—both of which are thought to be spiritually powerful symbols. On Easter day, people visit relatives and friends and give them Easter baskets filled with cake and eggs.

First Week of May

The first week of May is a holiday for the entire country of Ukraine. Two holidays are celebrated at the beginning of May.

Labor Day • *May 1*

Also called May Day, this holiday was one of the biggest celebrations of the year under the Soviets. Although it is still a public holiday in Ukraine, there aren't many parades or worker demonstrations anymore. People take advantage of the day off work to have some time to themselves.

Victory Day • *May 9*

Almost every family in Ukraine suffered tremendously under the Nazi occupation during World War II. This public holiday honors the memory of those who were lost with large military parades, wreaths and flowers placed of the graves of those who died during the war, and fond remembrance of loved ones lost. The few remaining veterans of the fight during World War II will wear some symbol of their uniform, such as a hat or medals.

Holy Trinity Day • *Fifty Days after Easter*

This religious holiday celebrates the Orthodox Pentecost, the day when the Holy Spirit descended on Christ's apostles, who were then able to speak in many languages so all visitors to Jerusalem could understand them. People decorate their homes with greenery, a symbol of new life. During a festive church service, wildflowers are blessed, dried, and kept behind the statues and holy pictures in the church because they are thought to have special power. Putting dried flowers above the door is thought to protect a house from fire.

Constitution Day • *June 28*

On this day, people celebrate the signing of the Ukrainian Constitution in 1996. Traditions are still developing for this new holiday. Some cities, for example, hold concerts. The Hymn of the Ukraine will be broadcast and sung everywhere in the country.

Independence Day • *August 24*

This holiday is the equivalent of America's Fourth of July. It celebrates Ukraine's independence after the fall of the Soviet Union in 1991. As in America, people celebrate this day with military parades, festivals, and family get-togethers.

Day of Knowledge • *September 1*

This first day of school for students at all levels gets the new school year off to a great start! Different celebrations are held for each level of student, depending on their age. This holiday is especially fun for grade school kids who bring flowers for their first teacher and gather in the school yard for the first ringing of the school bell that opens the new school year.

City Day

Each Ukrainian city has a fun City Day (or two!) that honors when it was founded. How each City Day is celebrated varies from town to town. But the festivities can include performances, concerts, fireworks, and decorating the streets.

Creative Arts

Music and Dance

Folk Music

Despite the former Soviet ban on all things Ukrainian, Ukrainian folk music has been well preserved and thrives today. Every event in life—weddings, funerals, holidays, birthdays, the harvest—has its own special songs. In recent years, groups have formed throughout the country to preserve this important part of Ukrainian cultural heritage. Even well-known Russian composers like Peter Tchaikovsky, who wrote such famous pieces as *Swan Lake* and *The Nutcracker*, collected and used Ukrainian folk melodies in their works.

Folk Dance

Ancient Ukrainian dances were agricultural dance games usually performed in a circle, which was associated with the sun. Most of the Ukrainian folk dances still involve this circular movement, accompanied by a song.

As with Ukrainian folk music, there are folk dances for every event. Each region has its own dances. Some are performed only by women and some only by men. And with some, everybody gets into the act—with the dance steps representing events that occur in everyday life. The women in Ukrainian folk dance have a very traditionally feminine role. They dance gracefully and modestly.

Folk Instruments

Ukrainian folk music gets its distinctive sound from several types of instruments, including lutes and flutes, the violin, the bagpipes, the drum, and the tambourine.

The hurdy-gurdy is a mechanical violin you've probably never seen but might have heard in folk tunes or even in modern music. It resembles a fiddle. The strings make a sound by passing over a wheel that functions like a violin bow. The musician turns the crank on the wheel and presses wedges on a keyboard against the strings to change their pitch.

The Soviets had once banned the hurdy gurdy because traveling musicians were playing them in the city streets, often including religious tunes. Today the hurdy gurdy is popular again—especially in folk song groups.

Folk Costumes

Much of the Ukrainian folk dress has its roots in the costumes of ancient times, but is rarely worn today except for performances, for festive occasions, and for dressing people being prepared for burial. Those who do wear folk costumes are much more likely to live in the countryside since urban Ukrainians dress like Westerners.

The folk dress that remains, however, is beautiful and colorful. Each region has its own costumes. Women's costumes include elaborate headdresses; long, colorful skirts; embroidered blouses; and vests. Men's costumes include woolen coats; long, tunic-like shirts; and a high felt hat.

Folk Art

Despite the almost constant upheaval in Ukraine over the decades, one thing has remained: the deep love of hand-crafted things.

Wood Carving and Decorative Painting

Ukrainians have always decorated their homes with folk art. Like their dance and music, they create hand-made items to celebrate every aspect of their lives. They also hand down their traditions in Easter egg painting, weaving, wood carving, decorative painting, and needlework from generation to generation. This assures that folk art is—and will stay—very much alive in Ukraine.

Go into any home, and you're likely to see wooden containers or porcelain vases decorated with scenes from folklore. Flowers, which symbolize love for country or a woman's physical beauty, might be painted on vases or embroidered onto shirts.

Easter Eggs

Decorative painting is also seen in *pysanki,* the colorful Easter eggs that are the traditional symbol of fertility. Designs are drawn onto the eggs with wax. The eggs are dyed bright, beautiful colors. But the color is not absorbed into the wax pattern. When the entire egg is dyed and cooled, the wax is removed and only the pattern remains. According to legend, the painted eggs formed out of Christ's tears. People still see these eggs as a protection from evil.

Weaving

Ukrainian weavings and tapestries are some of the world's finest. Whether weaving clothing, coverlets for the bed, or wall hangings, the depth and intricacy of Ukrainian weavings are breathtaking. Some of the items are made of wool, silk, and even imported gold and silver threads. The silk and the metal threads give a beautiful shine to the piece. Before the 1800s, all tapestries were hand woven on vertical or horizontal looms. A good weaver could produce several yards of fabric in a day.

The State Museum of Decorative Folk Art in Kiev has one of the largest collections of Ukrainian folk art in the world.

Folk Architecture: Wooden Churches

In many parts of Ukraine, there was no stone for construction, so timber was used instead—especially for churches. All Ukrainian wooden churches are built according to a similar design. Each had a nave (the central part of the building that leads up to the altar), with aisles on either side of it. Each was built in the approximate shape of a ship, oriented from east to west. The domes or spire reaching up from the roof was its mast, and the cross was its sail.

Initially, the central frame of each church was built in a cube shape; the designers could add additional cubes onto the building. The wooden planks were laid in vertically (up and down) instead of horizontally (across). The belfry (bell tower) was usually separate from the main church building.

The construction of Ukrainian wooden churches reached its peak in the 18th century. There are many of them in the country today, still in use, each one a bit different from the other. All of them are peaceful reminders of the country's long-standing folk traditions.

Castles

Ukraine's location at the crossroads of Europe and Asia made it vulnerable to invasion over the centuries. As a result, the country is filled with castles and fortresses. All of them are remarkable, considering the resources available when they were built. Some of the castles that were built for defense were later transformed into well-protected homes for the rich. Most of them were abandoned by the end of the 18th century, and some fell into ruin. Those that have been repaired and revitalized are magnificent.

Many Ukrainian castles blend in well with their spectacular surroundings. They were usually built on a hill where the whole countryside was visible so the castle could be defended from all sides. Some of them also served as prisons. Today, many of them are museums explored by tourists and locals alike. If you want to see spectacular Ukrainian craftsmanship in stone carving and gold-plating, Ukrainian castles are some of the finest in the world.

Swallow's Nest Castle

Sports & Games

Sports

During the Soviet era, there was much emphasis on physical education. As a result, there are many athletic facilities, swimming pools, and playing fields throughout Ukraine. Today, fitness clubs are popping up, too—another sign of Ukraine's Westernization—along with yoga and martial arts studios.

Football (soccer) is the country's most popular sport. Ukraine has four national football leagues. Together with Poland, Ukraine will host the UEFA (Union of European Football Associations) European Football Championship in 2012.

Ukrainians love racquet sports like tennis. Golf is becoming popular, too. The Great Outdoors call many Ukrainians to spend free time hiking and rock climbing. The beautiful waters attract scuba divers and everyone else who loves to spend time on and in the sea. The increasing amount of sporting goods coming into the country means more equipment to do more things. Ukrainians are getting into extreme sports like hang-gliding, bungee jumping, hot air ballooning, and skydiving.

Ukraine and the Olympics

Ukraine first went to the Olympics as an independent nation in 1994 at the Winter Olympic Games in Lillehammer. As of 2009, Ukraine has won 96 medals in four Summer Olympic Games and five medals in four Winter Games. 15 of those medals, including six gold medals, were in gymnastics.

The Ukrainian government bid Bukovel, a Ukrainian ski resort, to host the 2018 Winter Olympic Games. The International Olympic Organizing Committee will announce the winning bid in 2011.

Favorite Toys

Even though Ukrainian kids are starting to get the same high-tech stuff that kids all over the world have, like videogames and MP3 players, they still love hand-made toys.

Traditional Ukrainian wooden toys are just as appealing to adults as they are to kids. They are handcrafted by wood carvers from the Ukrainian forests, and no two pieces are alike. Flutes and whistles, wiggling snakes, and an eggy bank decorated like pysanki are just some of the treasures kids keep all of their lives.

Some people have matryoshka dolls that have been passed down from generation to generation. These nested sets of dolls are popular throughout Eastern Europe. There can be five or more dolls in a set. Each doll—not matter how small—is beautifully painted. Some artists create sets of doll with certain themes like fairly tale characters or animals. You can even order matryoshka dolls with themes that include Barbie, Disney characters, and the Simpsons!

"BIG BEAR IS COMING!"

This is a game of tag that Ukrainian kids play in the snow. You can try this in the snow. If you live in a warm climate, try it in the sand. If you don't have snow or sand, draw a large square with a piece of chalk. The square must be large enough for at least eight people to run around in.

Number of Players Needed
Up to eight

Materials Needed
- A large space outside with no obstacles
- A stick for drawing a large square in the snow or sand OR
- A piece of chalk for drawing a square on concrete

Directions
1. Draw a very large square on snow, sand, or the playground. The square must be big enough for eight people to run around in.

2. Draw a smaller square inside the big square. The smaller square is Big Bear's den. It must be large enough for eight people to stand in.

3. Choose one person to play Big Bear. This person stands inside Big Bear's den.

4. Big Bear yells, "Big Bear is coming!" and runs out of the den, chasing the other players. The goal is for Big Bear to touch another player within the larger square.

5. Once Big Bear touches a player, they both hold hands and return to the den.

6. Both players yell, "Big Bears are coming!" Still holding hands, they run out of the den together and try to tag another player in the larger square. The newly tagged player returns to the den with the other two. They all hold hands.

7. Players must hold hands as they run out of the den and tag other players, one at a time. This continues until only one player is left. This last player is the new Big Bear for the next game. If you decide not to play again, this last player is the winner!

Ukraine – MP5126

Name _____ Date _____

MAKE MATRYOSHKA DOLLS WITH A MODERN THEME

Nested matryoshka dolls have been traditional toys in Eastern Europe since the 1800s. Many artists today are putting a new twist on traditional themes. It's not uncommon today to see matryoshka with politicians, movie stars, rock stars, and popular TV characters.

Materials
- Magazines, the newspaper, and/or pictures from the Internet
- Glue
- Scissors
- Items of your choice: colored pencils, colored markers, sequins, glitter

Directions
1. Choose a favorite theme that interests you. Some suggestions include:
   - Characters from your favorite TV show or movie
   - Characters from a favorite book
   - Favorite musicians
   - Current politicians
   - The American First Family
   - The British royal family

2. Using magazines, the Internet, or other print sources, find four separate faces to paste onto each doll outline (provided on the next page). If you like to draw, you can draw the faces instead.

3. Finish each outline by drawing in the rest of the doll.

4. Display your matryoshka!

Doll Outlines

146

Ukraine – MP5126

ANSWER KEY

BELARUS

Plants and Animals of Belarus (page 7)

W	D	C	E	N	T	A	U	R	E	A
I	E	H	A	I	S	J	A	S	M	S
L	B	F	L	O	W	E	S	R	O	H
D	O	K	D	S	H	O	R	P	O	R
B	E	R	R	I	E	S	T	O	R	K
O	L	O	E	Z	A	H	U	T	H	A
A	K	G	O	A	T	N	R	A	S	O
R	E	V	A	E	B	C	K	T	U	D
B	I	S	O	N	L	H	E	O	M	P
F	A	L	C	O	N	R	Y	E	C	I
X	O	P	N	E	O	E	L	R	H	N
B	I	R	C	H	D	E	A	G	L	E
Q	A	K	N	I	T	D	E	I	A	T

CZECH REPUBLIC

Czech Idioms (page 31)

Answers might vary but should include most of the following. Allow non-native speakers to offer idioms from their home-country languages.

2. Buying things you don't need is just like **throwing money down the drain**.
3. The speaker had a **frog in her throat**.
4. If I get to the store and the post office before noon, **I kill two birds with one stone**.
5. The argument they got into was just a **tempest (or a storm) in a teacup (or teapot)**.
6. I looked outside, and it was **raining cats and dogs**.
7. Miguel knows Martin **like (he knows) the back of his hand**.
8. I'll **keep my fingers crossed** that your team wins the game!
9. Before James went onstage, his classmate whispered, **"Break a leg!"** for good luck.
10. Angelo **beat around the bush** instead of getting to the point.

Famous Castles of the Czech Republic (page 39)

K	D	Z	C	E	V	O	K	A	R	K
A	E	K	U	N	E	T	I	C	K	A
M	T	D	E	N	N	S	Z	W	A	R
E	S	M	A	R	R	I	P	O	U	L
N	I	R	O	K	O	K	V	V	V	S
N	P	O	U	N	V	O	K	O	S	T
P	O	R	E	P	O	R	S	I	O	E
R	N	E	S	Q	W	L	X	Z	Z	J
L	O	T	O	C	N	I	K	L	P	N
P	K	R	I	V	O	K	L	A	T	S
O	A	O	P	E	X	F	I	T	T	T
W	J	S	X	G	V	O	K	I	V	Z
R	Z	K	L	H	P	L	E	O	O	R
T	B	Y	P	W	D	E	P	D	A	A

GREECE

Greek Roots, Prefixes, and Suffixes (page 52)

Answers may vary but could include the following:
1. agriculture
2. athlete
3. democracy
4. sympathy
5. pediatrician
6. autobiography
7. geography
8. hyperactive
9. microscope
10. thermometer
11. biography
12. geometry
13. asteroid
14. biology
15. telephone

POLAND

Match the Polish and English Words (page 75)

1. G
2. N
3. J
4. A
5. L
6. B
7. I
8. C
9. K
10. D
11. M
12. E
13. F
14. H

ROMANIA

The Regions of Romania (page 89)

Answers about what each region is known for could include the following:

Banat	traditional German villages; mountain forests
Bucovina	painted monasteries
Crişana	medieval sites; resorts
Dobrogea	ruins of ancient Greek and Roman cities; resorts; Danube Delta
Maramureş	traditional wooden churches
Moldavia	historic cities; medieval fortresses; churches
Oltenia	monasteries; caves; health resorts
Transylvania	medieval castles and towns; forests
Wallachia	Bucharest; resorts; residences of Wallachian princes

What Did the Archaeologists Find? (page 93)

1. pottery
2. tool
3. bracelet
4. ring
5. hook
6. axe
7. statue
8. weapon
9. antlers
10. plow
11. wheel
12. stove
13. bone
14. coins
15. gold

ADDITIONAL RESOURCES

BELARUS

Books

Bryan, Nicol. *Chernobyl: Nuclear Disaster*. Milwaukee, WI: World Almanac Library, 2004.
Discusses the disastrous 1986 Chernobyl nuclear power plant accident in the Ukraine and its effect on neighboring countries.

Coffey, Wayne. *Olga Korbut*. Woodbridge, CT: Blackbird Press, 1992.
A biography of the incredible young gymnast who won three gold medals in the 1972 Olympics and another in 1976.

Gosnell, Kelvin. *Belarus, Ukraine, and Moldova*. Brookfield, CT: Millbrook Press, 1992.
Compares and contrasts the three former Soviet republics of Belarus, Ukraine, and Moldova.

Lerner Publications. *Belarus*. Minneapolis, MN: Lerner, 1993.
Discusses the history, geography, ethnic mixture, politics, economy, and future of the former Soviet republic of Belarus.

Web Sites

Belarus
http://www.belarus.by/en/
The official web site of the Republic of Belarus. Lots of cultural information on the country as a whole, including the arts and culture, sports, holidays, education, and famous Belarusians.

Belarus Magazine for You: Politics, Economics, Culture
http://belarus-magazine.by/en.php?
An illustrated monthly magazine about modern life in Belarus, including the people, traditions, culture, politics, and economy.

The Official Internet Portal of the President of the Republic of Belarus
http://president.gov.by/en/press10559.html
The official web site of the President of the Republic of Belarus. Includes a biography, photographs, and other information relating to the President.

CZECH REPUBLIC

Books

Roux, Lindy. *Czech Republic.* Milwaukee, WI: Gareth Stevens, 2004.
On overview of the geography, history, government, people, arts, foods, and other aspects of life in the Czech Republic

Taus-Bolstad, Stacy. *Czech Republic in Pictures.* Minneapolis, MN: Lerner, 2003.
A generously illustrated look at the Czech Republic.

Trnka, Peter. *The Best of Czech Cooking.* New York: Hippocrene Books, 2001.
Try some of these simple, delicious recipes!

Web Sites

Czech Republic
http://www.czech.cz/en?i=5
The official web site of the Czech Republic. Well-written, informative, and fun to read!

CzechTourism.com
http://www.czechtourism.com/eng/uk/docs/holiday-tips/news/index.html
The official travel site of the Czech Republic. Plan your trip!

National Gallery in Prague
http://www.ngprague.cz/en/1069/0/0/sekce/homepage/
Site of one of the main art museums in the Czech Republic. Check out the current exhibitions.

National Museum
http://www.nm.cz/?xSET=lang&xLANG=2
Site of the premier natural science and history museum in the Czech Republic. Check out some of the collections, including the Czech Puppets and Circus Exhibition.

GREECE

Books

Petersen, David, and Christine Petersen. *Greece* (True Books). Danbury, CT: Children's Press, 2002.
Includes lots of information about the country and resources for finding out more.

Evans, Lady Hestia, and Dugald A. Steer. *The Mythology Handbook.* New York: Candlewick, 2009.
An interactive book to help you explore the myths of Ancient Greece. Includes fold-out maps, postcards, and drawings. There is also a companion handbook.

Mitchell, Adrian, and Stuart Mitchell. *The Odyssey.* New York: DK Children, 2000.
A retelling of the epic poem, The Odyssey, *with illustrations and historical background.*

Osbourne, Mary Pope, and Natalie Pope Osborne. *Ancient Greece and the Olympics* (Magic Tree House Research Guide). New York: Random House Books for Young Readers, 2004.
Explores the first Olympic Games. Includes a guide for doing further research.

Pearson, Anne. *Ancient Greece* (DK Eyewitness Books). New York: DK Children, 2007.
Excellent overview of ancient Greece, including the Minoan and Mycenean civilizations, Greek city-states, Alexander the Great, gods, goddesses, heroes, temples, and festivals, foods, clothing, and jewelry.

Web Sites

Amanda Barrett's Greece for Kids
http://www.greece4kids.com/
Truly an insider's look at Greece! A guide for kids who go to Greece or want to know more about it, written by a grade school student who goes to Greece every summer. Filled with photos.

Ancient Greek Kids
http://greece.mrdonn.org/kids.html
Information about what it was like to grow up in Ancient Greece.

Olympic Team USA
http://www.olympic-usa.org/
The official web site of the U.S. Olympic Committee. Get information on America's Olympic athletes and find out more about the upcoming Games.

POLAND

Books

Browning, Christopher R., Richard S. Hollander, and Nechama Tec, eds. *Every Day Lasts A Year: A Jewish Family's Correspondence from Poland*. Cambridge: Cambridge University Press, 2007.
A collection of personal letters from those who lived and died in the Holocaust.

Deckker, Zilah. *Poland*. Washington, DC: National Geographic, 2008.
And easy-to-read overview of the land and people of Poland with special high-interest features that spotlight specific topics.

Haviland, Virginia. *Favorite Fairy Tales Told in Poland*. New York: HarperCollins, 1995.
Stories for readers of all ages.

Knab, Sophie Hodorowicz. *Polish Customs, Traditions and Folklore*. Rev ed. New York: Hippocrene, 1996.
Discusses the major Polish customs and traditions practiced over the centuries.

Lemmis, Maria. *Old Polish Traditions in the Kitchen and the Table*. New York: Hippocrene Books, 1996.
A cookbook and a history of Polish culinary customs. Short essays cover subjects like Polish hospitality, holiday traditions, and the mushroom. Included are more than 100 recipes for traditional family meals.

Singer, Isaac Bashevis. *Day of Pleasure: Stories of a Boy Growing Up in Warsaw*. New York: Farrar, Strauss and Giroux, 1969.
Singer won the Nobel Prize for Literature in 1978. This book includes episodes from his childhood in Warsaw, illustrated with old photos and focusing on Jewish life in the city.

Zuehlke, Jeffrey. *Poland in Pictures*. Minneapolis, MN: Twenty-First Century Books, 2005.
A well-illustrated overview of the geography and history of Poland. Pick out some places that you'll want to visit!

Web Sites

President of the Republic of Poland
http://www.president.pl/x.node?id=479http:/www.president.pl/x.node?id=479
The official web site of the President of the Republic of Poland. You can send the President an e-mail through this site!

Polishsite
http://www.polishsite.us/about-us.html
Features hundreds of articles about Poland, including customs, culture, history, lifestyle, and lots of other fun topics!

Polska
http://www.poland.gov.pl/
The official promotional web site of the Republic of Poland. Contains practical, historical, and cultural information.

ROMANIA

Books

Fernandez, Dominique. *Romanian Rhapsody: An Overlooked Corner of Europe.* New York: Algora, 2000.
Focuses on the warmth, beauty, and hidden treasures of Romania.

Klepper, Nicolae. *Romania: An Illustrated History.* New York: Hippocrene Books, 2003.
Tells the story of the evolution of the Romanian people, the creation of the Romanian principalities, their struggle against foreign powers, and their unification to form the state of Romania.

Simon, Ted. *The Gypsy in Me: From Germany to Romania in Search of Youth, Truth, and Dad.* New York: Random House, 1997.
The author travels 1,500 miles through parts of Germany, Poland, Russia, and Ukraine and finally arrives in Romania where he finds the roots of his Jewish parents and grandparents. His trip offers interesting sketches of life and culture in Eastern Europe.

Web Sites

Romania
http://www.romaniatourism.com/index.html
The official web site for Romanian travel and tourism. Lots of fun facts, history, folk lore, and practical information. Plan your visit!

Romania.org
http://www.romania.org/
A portal for the Internet's Romania content created by those who live in and/or love Romania.

Romania Simply Surprising
http://www.rounite.com/
Blogs from people who love Romania that are rich with information, beautiful pictures, and informed opinions on the country.

RUSSIA

Books

Afanasev, Aleksandr. *Russian Fairy Tales*. New York: Pantheon, 1976.
Nearly 200 traditional Russian folk and fairy tales in the only comprehensive edition of them in English.

Dabars, Zita, and Lilia Vokhmina. *The Russian Way: Aspects of Behavior, Attitudes, and Customs of the Russians*, 2d ed. New York: McGraw-Hill, 2002.
An insider's look at how Russians live, work, spend their free time, and observe holidays and customs.

Lychack, William. *Russia*. New York: Children's Press, 1996.
Surveys the sports and games played in Russia, with emphasis on the present day.

Massie, Robert K. *Nicholas and Alexandra*. New York: Ballantine, 2000.
Explores the doomed Imperial dynasty of Tsar Nicholas II and the Revolution that followed its fall.

Murrell, Kathleen Berton. *Eyewitness: Russia*. New York: DK Children, 2000.
This highly illustrated book includes geography, historical periods, and cultural topics.

Shulman, Sol. *Kings of the Kremlin: Leaders from Ivan the Terrible to Boris Yeltsin*. London: Brassey's, UK, 2003.
An insider look at the world of Russia's powerful leaders.

Web Sites

The Moscow Times.com
http://www.themoscowtimes.com/indexes/01.html
Web site of one of Russia's leading newspapers. Read news, opinions, blogs, and much more.

President of Russia Official Web Portal
http://kremlin.ru/eng/articles/about_siteEng01.shtml
The official web site of the Russian President's Office. Includes biographies of the Russian presidents, the text of the Russian Constitution, as well as the President's speeches and blogs. Also includes the history of the Kremlin (Russia's version of the White House). This site is just plain interesting! Check it out!

Russia Today
http://russiatodaytv.com/index.asp
Web site of Russia Today, Russia's award-winning TV program that highlights what's taking place in modern-day Russia in economics, politics, social issues, culture, and much more. Watch highlights of some of the shows.

UKRAINE

Books

Brett, Jan. *The Mitten.* New York: Scholastic, 1990.
This is a retelling of an old Ukrainian tale with beautiful illustrations. A boy drops his white mitten in the snow, and animals crawl inside it to get warm, one by one, until the mitten cannot hold one more.

Perchyshyn, Natalie. *A Kid's Guide to Decorating Ukrainian Easter Eggs.* Roseville, MN: Ukrainian Gift Shop, 2000.
Contains step-by-step instructions for decorating pysanky. Fun for people of all ages!

Reid, Anna. *Borderland: A Journey through the History of Ukraine.* New York: Basic Books, 2000.
Tells the story of Ukraine, combining facts and the author's personal experiences.

Weber, Valerie J. *I Come from Ukraine (This Is My Story).* Stamford, CT: Weekly Reader Early Learning Library, 2006.
A child's perspective on life in Ukraine.

Zuehlke, Jeffrey. *Ukraine in Pictures.* Minneapolis, MN: Lerner, 2005.
A beautifully illustrated look at Ukraine.

Web Sites

Internet Encyclopedia of Ukraine
http://www.encyclopediaofukraine.com/land.asp
Contains extensive information on the people, geography, economy, and cultural heritage of Ukraine. Written and maintained by the Canadian Institute of Ukrainian studies at the University of Alberta/University of Toronto.

Ukrainian Gift Shop
http://www.ukrainiangiftshop.com/index.htm
If you like Ukrainian Easter eggs, you'll love this site. It is the largest source of pysanky supplies in the world.

The Ukrainian Museum
http://www.ukrainianmuseum.org/about.html
Features lots of images from the museum's collection that focuses on Ukraine's cultural heritage. Plan your trip!

The Ukrainian Weekly
http://www.ukrweekly.com/index.htm
Publishes news about Ukraine and Ukrainians throughout the world.